THE LAST

Professor E. C. Wragg
Exeter University

Trentham Books

First published in 1996 by Trentham Books Limited

Trentham Books Limited
Westview House
734 London Road
Oakhill
Stoke-on-Trent
Staffordshire
England ST4 5NP

British Cataloguing in Publication Data
A catalogue record for this book is available from the British Library
ISBN: 1 85856 069 1

Acknowledgement
To Jonathan Hall for drawing the cartoons

Designed and typeset by Trentham Print Design Ltd., Chester
and printed in Great Britain by BPC Wheatons, Exeter

Contents

Foreword

Foreword

'Can it get worse?' was a common question amongst teachers as the last decade of the century opened. Well, it got both better and worse in the mid 1990s. When one loony policy ceased causing chaos, another took its place. Sir Ron Dearing's courageous attempt to simplify the national curriculum was a notable exception, a rare flash of intelligence in a period when tough guy statements were more important than substance.

As democratic procedures sailed out of the window, more and more decisions in education were made by unaccountable Quangos – the ever growing 'Quangocracy' as some called it. Alongside the power of the Quangos there was huge surge in the power of the Office for Standards in Education. 'OFSTED are coming' was what you whispered in the ear of any teacher or head suffering from constipation.

Yet despite the dreary bureaucracy most teachers managed to keep a sense of humour about what was going on. For some it was laugh or cry. Sadly the number of teachers retiring through ill health trebled within eight years. Many who stayed on were rescued by their colleagues' collective spirit. Teaching is a fabulous job when it goes well. What a pity that stress has taken the edge off the pleasure and satisfaction for some.

This is the eighth published collection of satirical essays I have written about education. I would never have thought, a few years ago, that school inspection would merit a section on its own. After all, Her Majesty's Inspectors had been around for 150 years, and had acquired a solid (or should I say 'generally sound'?) reputation for being the fair-minded evaluators of the system. That was before inspection became a profit-making business. OFSTED actually had to write to all its inspectors asking them not to tout for consultancy work when they were inspecting. I wouldn't have dared invent that as a piece of satire, but then, real life leaves satirists standing when it comes to tragi-comedy.

So will it get worse? I like to think that we have now plumbed the depths of the depths, and should slowly emerge blinking into daylight, but who knows how many more surreal comedians are lurking in the deep comic mine shafts from which they are excavated.

Ted Wragg

Chapter 1
Politics, politics

Save us from the legacy of all those twerps

Dear Gillian,

Your predecessors, except for John MacGregor, have been like a set of Russian dolls. Inside each one, waiting to emerge, was an even smaller twerp. The graph can only go up. Your first assignment is to repair the damage wrought by them.

Keith Joseph worked hard and rescued vocational education. Sadly he also rubbished teachers, which killed off numerous voluntary out-of-school activities. Goodwill is invisible, like the helium in a balloon – only when it has gone can you can see what it did.

Kenneth Baker was the first of three of your forerunners to come in with 'liberal' credentials. It was a disaster. Baker, Clarke and Patten spent all their time bellowing 'Me Tarzan', to persuade the Right Wing they were macho. And don't bother reading Kenneth Baker's autobiography *Was I Bloody Brilliant or Was I Bloody Brilliant?* – although it was better written than a Jeffrey Archer.

It was Margaret Thatcher's mistrust of teachers that buried them under so much Government-imposed bureaucracy. In the 1988 Education Act, Baker took over 400 additional powers. You should shred these. The Government now decides exactly what is taught, even how many beads are counted out by seven year olds in national tests, or how the register is filled in. R A Butler, who believed politicians should stay out of the classroom, has been turning in his grave these last six years.

Kenneth Clarke propagated the philosophy of the Dog and Duck saloon bar. The chapter on education in his autobiography should be called 'He Came, He Went'. Never one to waste time on reading, he demolished Her Majesty's Inspectorate, saying that a butcher could inspect a school, introduced disastrous teacher training 'reforms', and slid off. His brief sojourn left you many fences to repair.

As you stroll by the fountains of the ludicrously over-ornate Sanctuary Building (beware, no secure haven here), which houses the renamed Department for Education (as opposed to the Department

1

against Education presumably), you will notice bird droppings on its pantomime-set plants. The air is thick with John Patten's pigeons coming home to roost.

He insulted the national representatives of parents, supposedly central in Government policy, calling their views 'Neanderthal'. He alienated teachers even more than previous ministers – quite some feat – had national test boycotts, infuriated heads at their annual conference, saying he was too busy to answer questions. There were other blunders. Pretend you don't know him.

So there is a lot for you to do. You could start by making sure the National Curriculum, currently set out in 30 to 40 dense folders, really is simplified. We have the most prescriptive curriculum in Europe.

Next you must sort out national testing. Do not stake all on league tables. When some highly selective school comes top of the league and a school for children with learning difficulties comes bottom, what has this told us?

The Office for Standards in Education, OFSTED, or OFFTHEWALL as it is known, runs a 'free market' in inspection. Retired technology advisers and Mafeking veterans now inspect schools for profit. No one is tendering for small primary school inspections, there is no money in it. OFSTED reports are all written to a mechanical formula with meaningless terms like 'generally satisfactory'. Reform OFSTED – soon.

Two final points: stop giving grant-maintained schools backhanders, when 90% of our children do not attend them and secondly, kill off the quangos that now spend billions of pounds and are unaccountable to anyone other than yourself. Do not pack them with ranting right-wingers.

If you want a standing ovation after your speech today, say you will bring back caning, that teachers are Marxist loonies, and decree hourly spelling tests. The applause will register 10 on the Richter scale.

But the 21st century is six years away. People may have thirty years of healthy retirement, so huge cuts in adult education are wrong. The free market does not replace the need for vision, values, co-operation and partnership. Hankering after imagined glories of the 19th century is no substitute for a vision of the 21st. Sock that to them Gillian.

Yours sincerely, Ted Wragg

Independent 13.10.94

Carry on cutting up the curriculum

January Schools are sent their glossy copy of the Dearing Report, the 'slimmed-down' National Curriculum, produced by Sir Ron Dearing. (The Government set fire to the curriculum, brought in the Fire Brigade when the flames were out of control, then congratulated themselves on dialling 999. This used to be called 'arson', and you were locked away for it).

Schools will ask if there is any money to buy the necessary books and equipment for this latest version of the National Curriculum. After all, the Government found cash for books for the General Certificate of Secondary Education in 1985-86 (General Election in 1987), and for the first version of the National Curriculum in 1990-91 (General Election in 1992), so it is worth a bid for 1995 (General Election in 1995-96?).

February A bad weather month which will not affect school sports. Since many schools have sold their pitches to a supermarket chain, inter-school scrabble will be able to proceed uninterrupted by snow.

The Prime Minister will remind schools that all pupils must play competitive team games. We shall have lost the Ashes by then, so cricket will no longer be classified as a 'competitive' sport. It will become part of 'drama'.

Scrabble, in which we still excel, will flourish, though the comprehensives will get no credit for this.

March Research is published showing that most inspections by the Office for Standards in Education (OFSTED), the privatised body that has virtually replaced Her Majesty's Inspectorate, concentrate mainly on bureaucratic matters, rather than the quality of teaching and learning.

The language of school inspections, 'Ofskrit', will officially be recognised by the United Nations as a language separate from English. (Nowhere else does the phrase 'generally satisfactory' occur with such irritating frequency).

3

Whole careers will be forged by people fluent in Ofskrit. Universities will offer joint honours courses in the School of Modern Foreign Languages for students wanting to study Ofskrit and 'Bakerspeak', the official language of the National Curriculum (examples: 'deliver the curriculum', 'fulfil attainment targets', 'flangify your flidgets' etc)

April Teacher unions meet at the seaside and threaten to boycott national testing. Gillian Shephard says this is regrettable and will make the league tables look funny (Pupils entered = 0, passes = 0, average score = 0.00, League position = 1st equal, along with 23,999 other schools).

One delegate at a conference utters the words 'I am a teacher, not a social worker'. If this doesn't happen it will be the first time since the Pharaohs.

May As schools gear up for national tests, GCSE, A-levels and vocational exams, a journalist spots that public exams coincide with the hay fever season. A doctor says that it can be treated, and thousands of pupils with streaming eyes will still sneeze their way through, despite the nasal sprays, eyedrops, antihistamine pills and chewed beeswax. Optimists propose switching exams to January, so everyone can have flu instead.

June As university final examinations finish, Dr Blandly Smiling of Élite Academy will say that 'more' means 'worse', that all students are short-haired layabouts, that when he was a lad they knew their tables up to a million times a million and could declaim the whole of the Aeniad off by heart, and that today they can barely spell 'Coronation Street' or count their housing benefit (there isn't any). While his students flog away through the Summer to earn money to pay off part of their £2,000 overdraft, he will then bugger off for three months of sunbathing and alcoholic haze in Tuscany, pretending that he is beefing up his department's research rating.

July Schools break for the Summer knowing, in many cases, that they must lose teaching posts and increase class sizes in September. The Government will say that there is no evidence that class size is related to school achievement (there is, but you have to get below 20 pupils to show gains, hence their lack of enthusiasm for the evidence).

Some politician will say that he was educated in a class of 60, beaten every day with a knotted bootlace, forced to run a 10-mile cross country in his wellingtons, and it never did him any harm (twitch, twitch). He will then go into Prime Minister's question time and shout abuse for an hour.

August GCSE and A-level results come out. Pass rates are up on last year. Entries at A-level in maths, physics and chemistry are down on last year.

Ministers initiate an enquiry into falling standards (in November they will say that higher pass rates are a triumph for their league tables policy). There is a rush to get into universities, which must hit their targets exactly, since they have cash taken away if they under-recruit and get fined if they over-fill.

Accountancy departments will be much easier to get into, as the 1980s yuppie bubble has now burst, but you will still need a hat full of grade As to secure a place in law, veterinary science and the posher universities. Two grade Es in knitting and bean growing will be enough to scrape into somewhere, if you (and they) are desperate.

September Back to school, with the political parties outdoing each other to boast about their nursery education plans (none will actually do anything).

A school will decide to take OFSTED to court, especially if one of the parents is a solicitor, over a critical school report. Previously schools were allowed to comment on the factual accuracy of inspection reports before they were released. Now reports are all over the press before anyone can say 'there are two 'r's in 'curriculum', but only one in 'you bastards'".

October An autumn reshuffle puts John Patten back as Secretary of State for Education (I'm only kidding, go back to sleep). Another Parent's Charter is produced at huge cost, but this time ready perforated for quick recycling. OFSTED starts inspecting Art Galleries (Rembrandt – 'above the national average', Titian – 'generally satisfactory', Toulouse Lautrec – 'didn't have regular assemblies', Monet – '17th in the league table').

November It's league table time again, sponsored this time. Gasworks Comp comes bottom of the Munchyburger Truancy League, having filled in its returns honestly. Slyville Academy comes top. The school logged off its daytime shoplifters as being on 'work experience'. The head of Slyville demands, and receives, a performance-related pay award. Proposals for performance-related bonuses for headteachers give top weighting for 'staying within budget', so heads decide to send the pupils home and fire all the staff.

The Scilly Isles come top of the Doggifood Local Authorities League again, so according to market forces 8,000,000 pupils will leave the rest of the UK and move to the Scillies, which then sink to the bottom of the Atlantic. That's the market for you.

December Christmas privatised – OFSTED inspectors bid for contracts to produce school Christmas plays. ('There were shepherds abiding in their generally satisfactory fields...'). *Carry on Education* is shown on BBC 1 on Boxing Day, with Kenneth Williams and Sid James as junior ministers, and then repeated in real life for the whole of 1996.

Independent 29.12.94

'Will this affect my performance related bonus?'

Treat yourself and tear it up, missus

It's a thick booklet, coloured blue. It must be from the Government. It's glossy and probably cost a fortune to produce. It really must be from the Government. It suggests that people in schools have lots of money to spend, are a bit gormless about how to spend it sensibly, can be gulled into selling a bit of land to a supermarket, and it mentions 'profit' at regular intervals. It's definitely from the Government.

Yes, it is indeed the latest belter from the Department for Education that has been thudding on to the mats of Flybynight Enterprises Inc and Arthur Daley Ripoffs Plc recently, an expensively produced 49 page thriller entitled *Education means business: Private finance in education*. The message dripping from every page is 'There are rich pickings out there lads'. With John Redwood apparently wanting to privatise Snowdonia, there is now no limit to loony right-wing market ideas.

Let me make it clear from the outset that I am in favour of positive education and business partnerships. There are good examples of benign collaboration, and many employers, schools and colleges have worked together to achieve these. I am right behind them. Education largely neglected the workplace in the 1960s and 70s, and sensible, mutually beneficial partnerships have been a considerable strength since that time. What I object to is the invitation in this blatant DFE propaganda to go out and pluck the turkey. The DFE pitch has all the subtlety of huckster-speak. 'Roll up, roll up. You won't believe what we've got 'ere. Tell you what, I like your face missus. Treat yourself. To you a tenner'.

First there is the Del Boy come-on: 'The education service has an existing capital stock worth £60 billion and public funding, both recurrent and capital, in the region of £25 billion a year....there are opportunities for any private sector company, large or small....The sort of partnerships that are possible will enable the private sector to profit both financially and in other ways from this large and relatively untapped market'. So are you with us thus far lads? Yum yum. Message number one reads: *These schools are awash with loot.*

The booklet moves to come-on number two: 'Another common factor is that recurrent funding is largely determined by pupil numbers. The more successful a school is in attracting pupils, the more funds it will receive. Schools therefore have every incentive to work together with the private sector in order to enhance their facilities'. Got that lads? You're home and dry. Message number two reads: *They are absolutely bloody desperate.*

Now for the sting: 'Schools are steadily moving from local authority control into the grant-maintained sector following a ballot of parents....Both grant-maintained and local authority schools provide attractive prospects for private sector investors....a developer might build a new facility in exchange for land owned by the school which it wishes to acquire, or schools might use facilities provided by supermarket operators in return for the firm's access to land forming part of the site'. Still with it lads? The glossy booklet seems to have omitted the fact that 23,000 schools have not opted out, but message number three reads: *They are so bloody desperate they might even sell you the sports pitches.*

Then comes the knockout blow, the repetition, yet again, that schools are useless at managing, and business is absolutely wonderful at it, failing to recognise how well schools have managed against the odds in recent years: 'Part of the benefit to schools of private investment will come from the introduction of professional and commercial attitudes to staffing and financial management'. Did you read message four lads? *They're completely clueless.*

Maintained schools offer 'a significant market for private sector enterprise', it says helpfully, and, in the case of church schools, the local diocesan authorities usually own the site and assets. So write down message number five lads: *The vicar's a cinch.*

My advice on some of these 'partnerships' the Government wants to encourage is stick with people you trust. Find out what is happening in places like Birmingham and elsewhere, where business partnerships are not ripoffs, but well worked out for the benefit of the community. Failure to read the small print could be disastrous.

'Sharing risk with the private sector is fundamental', trills the glossy blue booklet, 'Risks which a school or college could not afford alone become manageable'. Yes indeed, you said it DFE. 'Del Boy Enterprises' simply goes bankrupt and starts up elsewhere as 'Del Boy Investments'.

Meanwhile Swinesville School picks up the bill and fires some of its teachers to pay for it.

So don't swap valuable land for a few used supermarket trolleys and a bit of work experience for the pupils. The way education is often treated nowadays you'd probably get the trolleys with the wonky wheels anyway, and the pupils would end up stacking shelves. Don't believe some fast talking entrepreneur, who promises gold but delivers sand.

Businesses, quite legitimately, are there to make a profit. This is fair enough in the open commercial market, but quite wrong when it comes to profits versus pupils, shareholders versus parents and teachers. I do not believe it when someone says that such clashes of interest and priority will never arise. They may not in good times, but they certainly will in hard times. The Ashenlungs Tobacco Company will not be happy about anti-smoking posters, and the Poshpeople Leisure Corporation will earn more from executive squash players than the school five-a-side league.

I am tempted to produce my own glossy rival booklet to the DFE glossy, entitled 'The Reverse Ripoff'. It will say to schools that business is awash with money, so sell them your surplus national curriculum folders as 'Executive document holders' at £50 a time. There are gullible directors, incompetent managers, surplus assets, just waiting to be picked clean. None of this is true, of course, but when did truth come into it?

Times Educational Supplement 3.2.95

Ken gets lost in a fog on the Tees

The news that Kenneth Clarke had gone up to the North-east and congratulated Consett on the splendid productivity record of its steelworks, which had in fact been closed down several years ago, surprised nobody who remembered his impeccable knowledge of education when he was Secretary of State. Not reading his North-east brief properly could be added to a huge list of other things he never read, like the Plowden Report, when he claimed to have buried it; his own national curriculum levels, when he asserted, wrongly, that large numbers of seven year olds could not recognise three letters in the alphabet; and the Maastricht Treaty, when he was supposed to be debating it.

His observation that Consett's magnificent steel production (er, actually it's zero, Clarkie) had been achieved with fewer employees than previously (ie none, at the last count) would have crowned another immaculate performance from the rotund maestro, had he not trumped his own ace by admitting that he had confused Consett with Redcar. One hoped in vain that he would don his swimming trunks and plunge fearlessly into a slow breaststroke across the nearest empty field, believing it to be the North Sea. He never did know his Arnside from his Elstree.

Just think of the post-Dearing national curriculum levels that Clarkie *failed* to achieve. Take geography for a start. There is some doubt whether he could even be given a tick in his level 1 box: 'Pupils ... express their views on features of the environment of a locality that they find attractive or unattractive. They use resources provided and their own observations to respond to questions about places'. The English Attainment Target 'Speaking and Listening' looks equally dubious at level 1: 'Pupils talk about matters of immediate interest. They listen to others and usually respond appropriately. They convey simple meanings to a range of listeners ... and begin to extend their ideas or accounts by providing some detail'.

But it is in the field of history that he bombs most embarrassingly. This is not surprising, since history is a subject he claimed, when minister, had stopped about thirty or forty years ago. So it's 'Working towards level 1' for Clarkie, as he fails gloriously once more to fulfil the level 1 rubric: 'Pupils recognise the difference between present and past in their own and other people's lives. They show their emerging sense of chronology by sequencing a few events and objects ... They know and recount episodes from stories about the past'.

The episode reminded me of Franz Kafka's novel *The Castle*, often regarded as a prediction of the modern bureaucratic state which turns human beings into ciphers. A Land Surveyor turns up by invitation to do some work at the Castle, only to be told that no-one is expecting him. He spends the rest of the novel unsuccessfully trying to find out what has happened, and eventually receives a letter congratulating him on his good work, even though he has not done anything.

If anyone needed reminding of some of the horrors that would occur from Accrington to Zouch if every school opted out and education were effectively nationalised, then Clarkie's geographical dyslexia must have clinched it. Everything outside a one mile radius around the House of Commons would fuse together into a giant undifferentiated glob, with no clear distinction, in the minds of ministers, between Cumbria and Cornwall, Birmingham and Bromley, Doncaster and Disneyland. In the surreal world in which some national politicians operate, schools are interchanged with supermarkets, teachers are indistinguishable from tea chests, yesterday is today, and Redcar is Consett.

One of the arguments against local control is that some local authorities are badly run, or that some councillors are incompetent. While this may be true of a small number of usually notorious LEAs or individual local politicians, the vast majority are well motivated, far more in touch with and committed to the welfare of their communities than central government could ever hope to be. It was a central government agency that sent thousands of test papers and customs clearance papers for a handful of seven year olds on the Scilly Isles. Most local councillors would take the trouble to check out personally a dangerous road crossing outside a school on their local patch, something a Whitehall-based outfit is unlikely to do.

In any case, for critics of the down side of political control, it depends what kind of prat is involved. There are several quite distinct species, eagerly hunted by enthusiastic Pratspotters, who scour the countryside from Consett to Redcar, clutching powerful binoculars and wearing blue anoraks. Some prats do not realise what they are bogging up – *wallius ignorans*, some are petty and spiteful – *wallius malevolens*, others know very well what mischief they are causing – *wallius sapiens*. The 'prat factor' is a much more lethal issue in national than local government, as relatively little real power resides nowadays at town or county level.

I would personally prefer a much lighter touch from central government than we have had in recent years, with local authorities concentrating on their support role, which many have done well during hard times. It is a pity that the possibility of a national inspection and support service with strong local roots, such as was mooted a few years ago, never materialised.

Schools continue to struggle financially because Kenneth Clarke and the Government will not understand what it means in an individual school to be so hard up they have to sack teachers.

No-one bleeds in Whitehall at this sort of local tragedy, especially when keeping schools short of cash is part of a high-risk pre-election strategy to cut income tax. When Barings bank did a similar double or quits, it was called 'gambling on the future'.

If you have strong views about national or local control of education, then please write to: The Chancellor of the Exchequer, Level 1, Treasury Building, London (near Tokyo).

Times Educational Supplement 17.3.95

Conclusive proof of a tosh offensive

Is it not hilarious how keen politicians are to quote research evidence, or the lack of it, when it suits their purpose? You would think, when treasured policies are under attack, that politicians are bucking for the Nobel Prize, the respect they start giving to research findings. Suddenly people who have previously shown the curiosity of a gnat about what has been discovered though careful systematic enquiry, start demanding scientific proof. It is a miraculous transformation – Dopey to Isaac Newton in microseconds.

The sequence of events is always the same. The argument goes something like this:

Can we have some money for schools, they're a bit short?
There is no evidence that money and pupil learning are related.
There were several big American projects that established a connection.
*There is no **British** evidence.*
There were some British studies a few years ago.
*There is no **recent** British evidence.*
There was a British investigation last year.
There is no recent British study of the impact of extra money on the learning of nine year old left-handed female pole vaulters in single sex rural primary schools.

As someone who both does research and also reads a great number of research reports, I am touched by the belated rigour that politicians are now keen to apply to research findings. It is a brilliant ploy to scupper every single request for funding or staffing with the 'Show me the incontrovertible proof' response. There rarely is conclusive proof of anything in education, as there are few absolute certainties.

The latest use of this device comes in the fatuous argument from Gillian Shephard about class sizes. The only convincing way of providing 'scientific' evidence about the effects of class size on children's learning would be to round up a large pool of identical twins, put one of each pair in classes of forty and the other in classes of fifteen.

Meanwhile a group of identical twin teachers would also be split into two groups. They would use identical materials and methods, holding every other conceivable factor absolutely constant. Since the only difference between the two groups of pupils would be the numbers in each class, children's learning, assuming one could measure it accurately, would reflect the effect of class size. A touch difficult to achieve in the real world, methinks.

So the absence of 'conclusive proof' puts the issue of class size into a very large group of other matters for which no such scientific support is available, nor usually asked for. There is no incontrovertible research evidence that if teachers swung from the chandelier pupils would learn better. There is not a smidgen of objective proof that if head teachers break wind in assembly the quality of maths teaching will suffer. For that matter there was no scientific evidence, more's the pity, that choosing a succession of wallies as ministers would wreck the education system, but that didn't stop prime ministers doing it.

The evidence on class size is of different kinds. First of all there is actually some research evidence, mainly American. It seems that you have to get below twenty pupils for the effects to become apparent, but what evidence there is looks persuasive. Also people usually prefer small groups to larger ones. A few years ago an American university split up its large first year as an experiment. Half the students went into one large lecture group, the other half were in small discussion groups. When the researchers followed up the students later, not one person in the large group had opted to study the field any further, but several members of the discussion groups had chosen it as their major subject.

Then there is custom and practice, which is often, though not always, based on intelligent action. If class size doesn't matter, then why don't cabinet ministers ask the private schools that their children attend to step class sizes up to fifty? The Government in any case claims that sock-it-to-em traditional teaching methods are superior, and think of the money the parents would save in reduced fees.

Why don't people learn to drive a car in groups of 40 or so? Why do the selfish beggars insist on having a teacher apiece? Imagine the court case if people did learn to drive a car in large groups. 'I'm sorry I crashed into that bus in front, m'lud, but I was trying to remember the lecture we had on the position of the clutch'. 'I quite understand the defendant's little problem. Traditional teaching methods are always best, and there is no conclusive evidence that class size matters. Case dismissed'. I think not.

So I've gone off Gillian Shephard a bit. She seems to me to be a very nice person, and to have one big selling point – she isn't called 'Baker', 'Clarke' or 'Patten', which is an enormous plus in my view. On the other hand she is frequently described as having embarked on a 'charm offensive'. Fine. But a big smile and a warm handshake are poor substitutes for the loss of thousands of teaching jobs.

It is all very well to read stories in the press about how she is 'fighting tooth and nail' in the cabinet for education, but many schools have virtually no money for books, are making teachers redundant, and are seeing class sizes climb disastrously.

If she really feels strongly about what is happening, then she should stand up in the next cabinet meeting and say, 'Knickers to you lot. If you don't find some more cash for education, I'm going'.

There may be no incontrovertible scientific proof that this action would make any difference. But the evidence that teachers are fed up of charm and smarm, sick of harangues about being to blame, and insulted by tosh about class size being unimportant, looks rock solid to me. Rather like the brown smelly stuff that is regularly dropped on them.

Times Educational Supplement 9.6.95

Ooh, I know ... Gillian is really Sybil

Do you know any millionaires? The Queen? Richard Branson? The Sultan of Brunei? Well, if any of them happen to have a four year old child, then do let them know that Gillian Shephard will be giving them a voucher for £1,100 out of public funds so they can, if they wish, send their nipper to an exclusive nursery school in Mayfair.

As I listened to Gillian Shephard on radio, announcing this munificent bounty for private education, a more and more tantalising question tormented me. That voice. Who was it? It couldn't be Gillian Shephard. I thought she was far too fair-minded to line the pockets of millionaires at the expense of the poor. But which actress was playing the part?

It was infuriating. I knew the voice so well. I shut my eyes. Suddenly it was like one of those radio quizzes where you hear a snatch from a 1970s sitcom and have ten seconds to identify the comic actor. She droned on in that slightly nasal whine. Then it came to me in a flash. Yes, of course! I should have got it straightaway, since the series is being repeated. *Gillian Shephard is really Sybil Fawlty*, wife of manic hotel owner Basil. You laugh, but listen carefully in future.

It's true. Educational policy has now become a *Fawlty Towers* series. School buildings rot, thousands of teachers are sacked, heads look at their budgets and find that they have precious little cash for new books or equipment. Meanwhile Sybil Fawlty doles out millions of pounds of public money for wealthy parents to spend on private education.

Normally I would not begrudge one penny piece spent on nursery education. It is scandalous that we have had to wait so long for a flicker of action by any Government. Nearly a quarter of a century ago, Margaret Thatcher, when Secretary of State for Education, promised a nursery place for all three and four year olds whose parents wanted it. Her paper was called, ironically as it turned out, *A Framework for Expansion*.

Now we get the first lunge. It consists of potentially the biggest handout of public money to private education since the Government came to power, bigger even than the Assisted Places Scheme.

Instead of targeting areas in desperate need of public cash for education in general, and pre-school education in particular, Sybil Fawlty shoves zillions of quid into the grateful hands of every millionaire, mansion owner, film star or water board chairman looking for an exclusive pre-prep school. It would be tragi-comedy in the best *Fawlty Towers* tradition, were it not too obscene to show before the 9 o'clock watershed.

What is worrying is that this is a triumph for the right-wingers in the Conservative party, who have toyed with the idea of vouchers for many years. Most sensible and fair-minded members of the party rejected the idea as being of the loony market-mad right. It was turned down for schools in the early 1980s by the late Lord (then Sir Keith) Joseph, and also rejected in the later 1980s for higher education. This current flirtation with the market philosophy of the far right looks like being the thin end of what could be a very fat wedge, one that, driven far enough, would eventually signal the end of free education.

It is odd how the voucher scheme has translated from a left-wing to a right-wing idea as it crossed the Atlantic. The system of vouchers was first tried over 20 years ago in Alum Rock, St José, California, a poor area where half the pupils were Mexican-American. It was designed to give fairer opportunities to disadvantaged children. Poor children's parents actually received *more* money than the rest. No 'topping up' was allowed, so the better off could not get preferment for school places.

Anyone tempted to believe that vouchers offer a Utopian solution should read the evaluation of the voucher experiment in America. The scheme was carefully monitored by the Rand Corporation. The research conclusions were that voucher classrooms were strikingly similar to non-voucher classrooms. The bureaucracy was such that teachers were buried under an avalanche of meetings. Worse still, there were no differences in educational standards, so eventually the scheme was scrapped.

Now that Major has been re-elected leader and can only stay in power with the support of the right-wing, it is quite clear that voucher plans are being offered so he can flash his right-wing market credentials at his critics. It has not been widely noted, but in the manifesto that he produced during the leadership election, Major also promised to

17

increase incentives for schools to opt out, so look out for further bribes and what his supporters were calling barmy right-wing 'swivel-eyed' policies, as he frantically clings to power.

One even more tantalising question remains. If Gillian Shephard is Sybil Fawlty, then who is Basil, now that the brilliant John Cleese has retired from the role? Well, that much is obvious. It must be John Major himself. He has taken over education policy during the last few years. Think about it – the spidery angularity, the sudden switches from ashen faced correctness to manic craziness, the strangulated tenor voice. Alright, so he has grey hair and glasses, and appears calmer, but then it is twenty years since *Fawlty Towers* was broadcast. Major is post-menopausal Basil. Basil is the mad one. Sybil appears reasonable by comparison.

And if this re-make of *Fawlty Towers* is really an allegory of loony right-wing ideas in education, then Michael Portillo, tipped to succeed Major, might as well play the part of Manuel. Going round in total bewilderment, saying '*Qué?*' and 'I know nothing', just about sums up the whole *Fawlty Towers* scenario.

So don't forget to tell King Croesus, if you see him, about his eleven hundred quid windfall. It could be the first of many more from Basil and Sybil.

Times Educational Supplement 21.7.95

Agony aunt Ada has all the answers

Dear Aunt Ada,

I have a four year old child and I understand I am eligible for a nursery voucher worth £1,100. The fees for my child's current nursery, the Mayfair Academy for Young Millionaires, are £10,000 a term. Can I use my voucher to defray these? Secondly, how do I set about getting my voucher? I listened to Gillian Shephard's speech in the House of Commons, but I couldn't understand it, and I'm an executive on £500,000 a year (plus share options).

Ivor Fortune, Chief Executive, Ditch-Water Plc.

You can indeed use your voucher anywhere, Mr Fortune, and the procedures are simple, as Mrs Shephard said. Send away for an application form to the Nursery Giveaway Offer, Easy Street, Bribeswork. Fill in the form, remembering to sign the section at the bottom which states 'I acknowledge receipt of my £1,100 gift which I will spend in the private sector if at all possible, and I promise to vote Conservative at the next election'. Mail the form to the DFEE (Department for Extra Enticements), who will send you a voucher to be spent on pre-school education, or any family holiday on the Costa Blanca.

Dear Aunt Ada,

I am a parent trying to understand the test results for 11 year olds announced recently. The papers said that they showed standards were falling, but I thought this was the first year children had done them.

Bea Wildered, Lilliput.

You are quite right, Bea. This year's tests represent attempts to guess what a Level 4 should look like. Since they have no past, if the tests show that standards are falling, it must refer to the future. Next year's scores will be higher than this year's, as the imperfections in this first run are eliminated. According to the unique laws of educational physics, if you compare this year's scores with next year's higher scores, therefore, then standards are indeed falling, but in a backwards direction. When next year's results come out, if the scores are actually lower, standards must also be falling. Whatever happens, standards are falling. It's all very simple really.

Dear Aunt Ada,
I am a senior official at the Office for Standards in Education. Teachers and other people working in education are laughing at what I say. My helpful and neutrally phrased pamphlet 'See the Light, Turn to the Right' has been ridiculed, and whenever I give a lecture at a conference, people in the audience chuckle. Can you suggest what I can do to improve teachers' reactions to my speeches?
(Name and address supplied)

The best solution to your problem is to try talking out of a different orifice.

Dear Aunt Ada,
We have just had an OFSTED report which says that our assembly is illegal, but I thought it had all the correct ingredients, a hymn, a prayer and so on. We even stopped the deputy head playing his guitar and singing a Beatles song during assembly while the inspectors were here. So where did we go wrong?
Chris T Anity, Headteacher.

The law is quite clear on this one, Chris. The Government does not allow Beatles songs in assembly, unless the text is changed, so 'Money can buy me love', 'With a little help from my bank manager', 'We all live in a blue submarine' are all permitted. Any school facing an opt-out ballot is not allowed to sing 'The magical mystery tour is waiting to take you away', as this is deemed to be subversive propaganda. Also you must intone the Government-approved responses at some point during your assembly. The head has to chant: 'May you teach well, no matter how big your class', and the staff must respond: 'Yea verily, for class size doth not matter'.

Dear Aunt Ada,
There has been a lot of talk in the press about the problems of teacher recruitment. Can you clarify the true state of affairs. How many teachers are retiring early, what level of applications are coming in for

new recruits, how many extra pupils are coming into school, and what does the future look like?
Worried Blue Eyes, Teacher Training Agency.

Early and ill-health retirements have gone up sharply in the last few years. Nowadays three quarters of teachers never make it to retiring age. Applications from trainees are well down, and since crazy proposals for the funding of teacher training are likely to be introduced soon, many training institutions are pulling out or reducing their intakes. As some 660,000 pupils reach 18 and quit schooling, about 800,000 children are coming in at the age of five, so school rolls increase by 100,000 or more each year. There should be no teachers at all by about 2020 AD, or possibly one teacher left, the last ever dinosaur, with a class of eight million pupils.

Dear Aunt Ada,
I am supposed to be Secretary of State, but the Prime Minister makes all the decisions about education on the basis of so-called 'advice' from right-wing think tanks. What on earth can I do? I am desperate.
G Shephard, DFEE.

Carry on doing what you have done so far, the message comes across very well – hold each official statement at arm's length, wear your glasses on the tip of your nose, then read it out in a mechanical voice, as if you know you are talking utter bollocks. Everyone understands.

Times Educational Supplement 9.2.96

Put a fresh spin on all that tough talk

I'm rough. I'm tough. I eat six inch nails and spit them out as cannonballs. You get in my way? Then eat lead, sucker. Go on, make my day. I'll show you. I'll .....

Oops! Sorry about that, only I was working on my new tough image. You see, those of us in education are clearly too wimpish. That is why the Government proposes hit squads and the like. The head has a cough? Bring in a hit squad. A teacher over there consoling some child who is upset? Fire the puny weed. From this moment on it's tough tough tough all the way for me, what is called the 'Now look here, sunshine' approach.

For those avid readers of documents on education who might have believed that dotty ideas have been elusive of late, I can assure you that rich and pungent sacks of them are still coming on to the market. The latest barrel load comes in a book by Peter Mandelson, reputedly a spin doctor by trade, called 'The Blair Revolution – can New Labour deliver?'. To which the answer is 'Hopefully yes, but not this kind of crap'.

Sit back and enjoy some of the toughest talk in town, as Pete spins a few belters in the *Guardian*. 'Schools require a new much tougher set of disciplinary sanctions to deal with unruly and uncooperative pupils ...'. (Go on, spin it Pete, talk tough. I like the cut of your jib. Let's hear you spin out the new tough school punishments, loud and clear) ' ... such as compulsory homework on school premises, weekend and Saturday-night detention, and the banning of favourite leisure pursuits such as attendance at football matches'.

Er, come again, Pete? I'm afraid I've spun out of control. I'm just picturing the family scene? The kids arrive home on Friday night. 'Right', says mum, 'Now Amanda, you'll need a fresh towel for swimming tomorrow'. 'Well actually, mum, I was talking in class, so the school has banned me from swimming this weekend'.

'Never mind' replies mum, 'you can go with your brother Billy and your dad to watch the United match in the afternoon'. 'Thanks, mum, it's a nice thought, but unfortunately Billy was laughing in assembly, so he's banned from watching United for two weeks'.

'Well, that's all right', mum persists, 'it's your birthday treat on Saturday night, and we're all going to the cinema'.

'Er, I'm afraid we've both got Saturday night detention, so we've got to go back to school'. Distant crunching sound as Amanda's dad rearranges head teacher's anatomy.

However, I don't want to be a wet blanket about these stunningly original and admirably tough ideas. This could be a first for Britain. So far as I know even the People's Republic of Albania does not let schools bar pupils from watching Tirana Rovers playing on a Saturday afternoon. I would much prefer to develop Pete's ideas further. There could be an agreed tariff of school offences, all named after the famous spin doctor.

A single Mandy Minor offences like illicit chatter, leaving your seat without permission.
Punishment: one shredded wheat for breakfast instead of two, and no toast.

A double Mandy More significant misdemeanours, such as underlining the date once instead of twice, or ruling a half inch not a one inch margin.
Punishment: only permitted to watch 'Grange Hill' with the sound turned off, no chips for a week.

A triple Mandy Even worse crimes, like splashing paint, or putting your bag in the aisle so someone will trip over it.
Punishment: not allowed to feed the goldfish, forced to go to the Fulham versus Torquay United match.

A quadruple spinning Mandy Heinous villainy, such as sticking chewing gum on the underside of the desk, or seeing who can piddle highest up the wall in the boys' toilets.
Punishment: Saturday all-day detention for compulsory PE, spinning round and round the gym for a few hours.

If there is a change in Government, then the one thing the whole nation needs is a dramatic change in tone and style. The macho assumption that, willy nilly, state 'toughness' is always best, whether with teachers, children, or society at large, is manifest garbage. Acting tough should be saved for when it counts, not be the first line of defence.

I blame Margaret Thatcher, who deluded herself that she got Government off our backs when the opposite was the case. Her deep distrust of her own colleagues, and of professional groups like teachers and doctors, led to a climate of deep suspicion instead of partnership, so what followed was inevitable.

The first national consequence was a macho style of management, in which professional people had to be told, by prats like Kenneth Clarke, exactly what and what not to do. Hence the endless bureaucracy and form-filling, as teachers, doctors, and other groups, in the absence of trust, are compelled to write everything down for inspection.

The second inescapable result was a proliferation of crackpot unworkable policies. Since the professions are scorned, advice is sought outside them, so any barmy think tank or pressure group, instead of being shown to the nearest padded cell, is given greater credibility than teachers and doctors. The latter are seen as 'vested' or 'producer' interests, while the former, however daft, are said to be the true voice of the consumer.

The third and most unpleasant outcome has been a general climate of stomach churning conflict, instead of harmony and partnership. This must change as the 21st century dawns.

So spin away, Mandy. Spin tough when necessary. But don't set teachers against families, when both are supposed to be on the same side. Try asking one or two practitioners for a bit of informed advice. It wouldn't come amiss after all these years.

Times Educational Supplement 22.3.96

Opt out, you lot, and be quick about it

For my money two of the best satirists on television are John Bird and John Fortune. Their brilliant deadpan sketches between the fictitious, but incredibly lifelike Government figure 'George Parr', and the television interviewer, have just been repeated on Channel 4.

It is a marvellous format, and the dialogue is full of irony, as the hapless George Parr often realises in mid-sentence the monumental daftness of what is going on. The two Johns have sometimes tackled education, with considerable success, so I have been wondering what George Parr might be up to nowadays.......

'George Parr, you're the architect of the Government's education policy. Could you, I wonder, just explain to us the logic of it'.

'I'm sorry. For a moment there, I thought you said 'logic''.

'I did'.

'Ah yes. Well, you see, it's all quite simple really. The Government believes in parental choice. That's why we allow parents to vote for their school to opt out of local authority control and go grant-maintained. And it's been a great success. Tremendously popular'.

'But I thought only a thousand schools have actually opted out'.

'Yes. It's been tremendously popular, a great success'.

'And 23,000 schools have voted not to opt out – so that's only four per cent of schools that did actually opt out in the last eight years'.

'Yes, It's been tremendously popular in the four per cent that did opt out. So popular in fact that Mr Major would like to see our policy of parental choice extended'.

'Extended?'

'Yes. We want all schools to opt out'.

'But what are you going to do about the 96 per cent of schools that have voted not to opt out?'

'We're going to compel them'.

'Compel them?'

'That's right. It's got to be done by parental choice, you see. So we'll just have to compel them to choose to opt out. It's what we call 'compulsory volunteering' – a bit like national service – which some of us would like to bring back, incidentally, for all those awkward long-haired layabouts who won't vote for opting out. But of course, the most exciting thing is that, when all schools have opted out, the Prime Minister wants them to select the best pupils, so they can all become grammar schools if they want'.

'But I thought the grammar schools only took the top 20 per cent or so of the population. So what's going to happen to the other 80 per cent – that's about six and a half million children, isn't it?'

'Well there's no need to nitpick about it'.

'Yes. Now, George Parr, another of your plans is to cut down on truancy'.

'Indeed. If children are not in school, how can they learn? We're determined to enforce discipline in schools, so anyone who plays truant will be dealt with most severely'.

'So what will happen to children who play truant?'

'They'll be expelled'.

'But if they're expelled, won't they just hang around shopping centres and get into trouble?'

'That's right. But we've got to have something to do for the extra 5,000 police officers we're planning to recruit. So they can arrest the little buggers, that'll keep them busy. And of course, this will help bring down class sizes'.

'Class sizes? Ah yes. The Government cut back the money for education, so schools had to sack teachers and class sizes got bigger and bigger'.

'No. Let's be quite clear about this. They were no education 'cuts'. Definitely no cuts....There were a few 'savings in public expenditure', but no cuts'.

'Savings?'

'Yes – 'savings' – or rather 'efficiency gains' as we like to call them'.

'So in what sense is sacking teachers an 'efficiency gain'?'

'Well, some of them might join the police force, for example'.

'So then, they could arrest the pupils who're playing truant because the classes are too big'.

'Exactly. I couldn't have put it better myself. And here's another example of efficiency gains. As Michael Heseltine has said, we're absolutely determined to cut back on all this dreadful bureaucracy going into schools. Do you realise, teachers are buried under so much paper – pamphlets and prospectuses, glossy brochures, silly demands of one kind or another – they've got no time to teach the children? It's dreadful, an absolute disgrace'.

'So who's sending them all this useless paper?'

'Well we are, actually'.

'I see. So what will you do with any money that you save from these efficiencies?'

'Well, this is something we're very excited about. You see, the Prime Minister is very keen on One Nation Toryism. So we're going to save £100,000,000 from the state school budget and give it to the private schools through the Assisted Places Scheme. One Nation. Take from one to give to another who needs it. A bit like Robin Hood'.

'But he stole from the rich to give to the poor, and.....'

'Yes, we're going to try it the other way round for a change – take money from the poor schools and give it to the rich ones – balance things up a bit. You see it's all part of our policy of choice and diversity. The state schools must compete with the private schools, so they must have choice and diversity'.

'So on this key issue of choice and diversity then, who actually decides what curriculum a state school can teach?'

'The Government'.

'And who decides what national tests children have to do?'

'The Government'.

'And who decides the financial formula for how much money schools get?'

'The Government'.

'So ..... there isn't much choice, and there doesn't seem to be too much diversity'.

'Well if you're going to split hairs, I suppose not'.

'George Parr, thank you very much'.

Times Educational Supplement 5.4.96

Shephard accentuates the negative

I have gone right off Gillian Shephard. When it is a matter of political survival, the gloves come off. Forget the 'charm offensive', and the 'let's be nice to teachers' resolutions. I have been watching her face grow harder, greyer and flintier, as more and more twaddle passes her lips in the interests of propping up John Major and coping with the loony Right.

I thought Gillian Shephard was better than that. After the bleak years of Baker, Clarke and Patten, there was a hope that she would give the teaching profession fair treatment, but when political futures are at stake, certain things go out of the window. Whoooosh! Goodbye to the smile and the warmth. Swishhhh! That was a few scruples and principles disappearing into the ether. Crash! There goes what little is left of the truth nowadays, shattering the window beyond repair.

The report on standards of reading in three London boroughs was presented to the press as an indictment of progressive teaching. This was Gillian Shephard repeating the interminable litany of the right-wing, when she knows it is tosh. Back in the good old days, the story goes, there was a Golden Age. Children sat in large classes, teachers told them the facts. As a result they could all spell every word in the dictionary, knew all their tables up to a billion times a billion, and could recite every cape and bay from Southend to Cape Squinxx on the planet Pluto.

The truth of the matter is that this 19th century style of education produced an ignorant peasantry, unknowing about science and many other aspects of life, and hating school with a deep intensity. Even the brightest did not achieve as brilliantly as the right-wing would have us believe. The D streamers in grammar schools were rubbished and, like John Major, often quit before A-Level, even though they were amongst the cleverest in their area. Under ten per cent of the population went on to higher education. Nowadays their equivalents, alongside thousands of others who would have failed the eleven-plus, are in that third of the population that goes to university.

After a thousand French lessons up to O-Level, our brightest pupils would eventually come face to face with a customs officer in Calais, asking them in French if they had anything to declare. Most were incapable of replying much beyond '*Il pleut*', or '*La plume de ma tante est sur la table*'. How many ended up paying customs duty on their Aunty Edna's biro is not recorded.

So are teachers 'trendies' who do not care about children learning? Not according to the much-altered first draft of the report on reading standards in three boroughs. Inspectors originally wrote, in one of the passages that was later deleted: 'Overwhelmingly, the teachers involved in this survey present themselves as pragmatic, non-doctrinaire people who want to have at their disposal the highest possible repertoire of skills and knowledge about teaching reading'. Not exactly a gang of raving, off-the-wall 1960s hippies.

It was alarming to see the alterations that appeared in the report and the spin that this gave towards the negative. A sentence like 'The quality of teaching of reading was satisfactory or better in approximately two-thirds of the lessons observed in Year 2', became 'in just one-third of these the quality of teaching was unsatisfactory or poor'.

It all made me wonder how you could reconceive the world and its heroes, if you pursued the same line. Take our great 20th century hero Winston Churchill. On the 'stress the negative' principle, people could say that he lost the first third of the war. Winston Churchill, the man who ran away from Dunkirk? I think there are better things to remember him by.

Then there is our 1966 not-so-great game in the football World Cup in 1966. England gave away a silly first goal, and then allowed Germany to equalise through bad marking in the last minute of ordinary time. The score? Oh yes, we won 4-2. But that confirms, of course, that, like teachers, we were one-third bad, rather than two-thirds good.

The Arts are no better. Culture is a huge flop if you take the Gillian Shephard view of life. Why did Michelangelo paint the ceiling of the Sistine Chapel? I get a stiff neck every time I go in there. And have you listened to Beethoven's Fifth Symphony lately? I've watched the orchestra and some of them do nothing for about a third of the time, they just sit there nursing their instruments. Why did Beethoven only write nine symphonies anyway? That is barely one every four years of his adult life. What was the lazy beggar up to?

We must aim for the highest levels of achievement for all pupils, especially those who desperately need a flying start in an important field like literacy. Sadly the inspectors did see some poor teaching. As in other professions not every teacher is ultra-competent.

It is not 'progressivism', however that may be interpreted, that is at fault. I have watched and analysed hundreds of lessons and seen good and bad teaching of all kinds. The simple recipe 'progressive equals bad, traditional equals good' is bunk. Someone droning on purveying inaccurate facts, is a 'bad trad'. A teacher who lets children do whatever they want, whether or not they learn anything, is not a progressive teacher, but a bad teacher.

Over the next few months, as the general election draws nearer, Gillian Shephard will be under pressure from John Major and the loony right to hammer teachers. It is an easy headline to earn. Some politicians believe that the public welcomes this scourging of their children's teachers, but my impression is that many parents do not like to see teachers done over ruthlessly. Perhaps she will only play it one-third dirty.

Times Educational Supplement 31.5.96

We're a long way down the slippery slope

Have you ever wondered what teaching will be like in the future? Then stand aside and let Gillian Shephard write your lesson plans. If politicians have their way, teaching methods will be prescribed, rather than teachers be allowed to make their own decisions. Unnecessarily alarmist? Well listen to this salutary story.

Back in 1980 I wrote an article entitled 'State-approved Knowledge? – Ten Steps down the Slippery Slope'. It described ten stages that would be needed for the state to have a complete grip on what was taught in schools.

At that time, before the introduction of the national curriculum, we only had the first step, centrally prescribed broad aims, such as 'help pupils develop lively, enquiring minds'. It was self-evident candy floss that only psychopaths would oppose, as harmless as saying that Tuesday should follow Monday.

At a national conference, a senior Government adviser said that I was being 'unnecessarily alarmist', as the Government had no intention of going beyond step three, 'an agreed syllabus'. In 1996 we now have seven of the ten steps fully in place, with prescriptions about syllabus, tests, league tables, and legal compulsion to teach what the Government of the day determines. The missing three steps are centrally prescribed teaching materials, remedial programmes and teaching strategies.

You only have to look at the pronouncements of leading politicians to see the temptation to tell teachers how to teach getting stronger by the hour. The tactics employed follow well-trodden routes. Stage 1: tell the public that schools are failing. Stage 2: attack teachers for incompetence. The third stage then appears logical, for if teachers cannot teach, they have to be told what to do. Kwality with a Kalashnikov. Simple, isn't it?

Tony Blair made a speech about the need for setting instead of mixed ability grouping, in which he specifically stated that this was not a matter for the Government to decide, but for the professional judgment of teachers. However, the spin doctors made sure that the impression given to press and public was that schools would be told what to do.

Gillian Shephard was much less subtle. She turned her attention instead to teacher training, a clumsy way of demeaning experienced teachers, because it wrote them off as a lost cause. I get just as fed up with attacks on teacher training as I do of attacks on teachers. Most teacher trainers are highly skilled at analysing lessons, courses have been 'reformed' every couple of years, and surveys show that over 90% of heads are pleased with the newly qualified teachers they have appointed.

It is interesting to see the tactics politicians are using to get control over teaching methods. Kenneth Baker developed them, as every one of his speeches was a triumph of tone over substance. He was always 'ploughing on to the end of the furrow'. Never mind what the furrow actually was, or where it led, or whether he ploughed up the dining room carpet by mistake. The tough-sounding tone was the thing.

The secret is the Three Word Trick. You select a word from each of three lists. The first list is verbs, the second adjectives, the third nouns. So in list one you pick a macho verb, such as 'enforce', 'compel', 'determine', 'order', 'impose', 'demand', 'require'. List two offers powerful adjectives, like 'tough', 'rigorous', 'complete', 'searching', 'far-reaching', 'strong', 'firm'. The third list is of impressive-looking nouns, such as 'discipline', 'scrutiny', 'performance', 'standards', 'achievement'. There are no weasel or wimpish words, like 'reflect', 'care', or 'consider'.

The method is dead easy. Look out for numerous examples as the general election approaches. Perm any three and you get gems like 'We shall impose tough standards', or 'The Government will demand firm discipline'. It's a great game, and anyone can play. The only problem comes if you get the words a bit mixed up and say 'We shall demand rigorous and far-reaching netball', or 'I will impose tough art'.

But does anyone seriously think that teachers can be told, on a daily basis, exactly how to teach? Chris Woodhead says that maths lessons should consist of at least 60% whole class teaching. The research evidence on effective teaching is clear on one matter in particular, that there is no single omni-purpose 'good' way. It depends substantially on the context.

So if someone does impose a quota, what do you do if you run out of time? 'Er look Year 1, I'm afraid I've just gone over quota on 'whole class teaching', so if you sit quietly I'll just come and whisper 'Little Red

Riding Hood' into your left ear. It will take a while for me to get round to everybody...'.

Or could teachers be saying, 'Now, Year 10, pay attention. I'm going to ask you six questions, explain three key concepts, and then you've got, I make it, seven minutes and three seconds in your groups to write the hundred word Government-approved response to the question 'Are there such things as black holes?'.

Or perhaps even, 'Sound it out Jemima, because the Government says I've got to use lots of phonics, so let me hear you say h-i-c-c-o-u-g-h equals 'huhickerkerohuggerhuh', nice and clear now. A funny word? Yes, it's a Martian expression meaning 'a complete prat".

Of course the official response to the very suggestion that the Government is trying to tell teachers how to teach will be to deny it. 'Us guv? Would we be so silly as to tell teachers how to do their job? And how could we possibly enforce it?'. To which the answer is: wait until there is a Government-imposed teacher training curriculum and the Office for Standards in Education is asked to comment on the application of Government-approved teaching methods as part of every school inspection.

'Unnecessarily alarmist', as they said back in 1980.

Times Educational Supplement 28.6.96

'So how much whole class teaching would you say you do?'

Chapter 2
The Inspector calls

Crash, bang, wallop, what a creature

Bash! Take that you prat! Thwack! Serves you right! Smack! That's one in the eye for you, sunshine! Teachers are responsible for the holes in the ozone layer and my failure to win a single prize in the National Lottery, so – wallop! You got what was coming!

Oops, sorry about that. Only I was just bashing a few teachers. Gillian Shephard had declared a moratorium on teacher thumping, but the press coverage of Chris Woodhead's speech about progressive teachers smoked out the teacher bashers. As it has been reinstated as a national sport, I thought I'd don the steel toecaps and have a go myself.

I read Chris Woodhead's speech with interest. If progressive child-centred teachers are the major obstacle to raising standards, why did smart previous Senior Chief Inspectors never spot this? Eric Bolton dismissed his successor's suggestion that teachers do not want to teach subject matter, saying 'It's ridiculous to believe that the process could grind away like a coffee grinder without a bean'.

But Chris Woodhead was so insistent about these allegations, he had three turns: an article in *The Times*, a speech, and his annual report. I love a debate about standards or teaching methods, and criticism of low expectations is very important. But I did wonder, Chris, if you'd read carefully your own inspectors' reports. After all, their report on reading, for example, did say that the vast majority of teachers use a mixture of methods.

I am also very confused about the origin of Chris Woodhead's current thinking on these matters. You see, Chris, one of the things we boring old professors of education sometimes do is check out original documents. I have been reading one or two articles written by someone called Chris Woodhead in this very newspaper a few years ago, and there do seem to be differences between that Chris Woodhead and what the present Chris Woodhead has been saying.

I shall illustrate. To avoid even more confusion let us call the earlier Chris Woodhead, who at the time was working in a university, training teachers, Wood Chrishead. Now a few years ago, if you remember Chris, your earlier incarnation, Wood Chrishead, wrote an article in *The TES* called 'Public Facts and Private Feelings'. It said things like 'Just as education itself has become a scapegoat for economic ills, so within education the arts subjects are having to bear the main brunt of the utilitarian attack'.

You must remember it Chris, because Wood Chrishead got quite impassioned. It was a very eloquent piece, as Wood laid about him: 'The economic recession might explain the present hardening of attitudes, the backlash against anything savouring of a progressive ideology' .... 'arts subjects attempt to explore the inner world of private feeling, whereas the curriculum as a whole encourages the successful manipulation of public fact'.

The reason I am feeling a bit confused, Chris, is that our friend Wood did sound a bit, well, er, progressive and child-centred. Just listen to Wood, now in full flow: 'It would be easy to swamp early and inarticulate fumblings after the right form with premature intervention' ... 'the pressure society puts on children to rest content in their prescribed roles as consumer puppets' ... "finding oneself in the world' at best means learning to use some of the skills and techniques of enquiry that underlie different forms of knowledge' ... 'Merely to echo the Festival of Light in their wilder moments is unlikely to produce any significant change in the quality and relevance of the work that goes on in schools'.

Then do you remember, Chris, another *TES* article by Wood Chrishead entitled 'Getting the Proper Attention'? An excellent piece, but not one that castigated progressive teaching. Quite the reverse. Again it seemed very, well, er, child-centred. Can you recall the content? A bit of an irony here. The kind of teaching Wood attacks is what the post-Dearing version of the national curriculum English document, supervised by his later incarnation, Chris Woodhead, seems to require under Attainment Target 2: 'Pupils should be taught to extract meaning beyond the literal, explaining how choice of language and style affects implied and explicit meanings'.

Wood wrote that after adults read a poem at home, like one does, we sit silently and think about it. 'What happens in the school English lesson? Do teachers allow for this private and silent period of thought? Far from it: in my experience we tend to open fire immediately, with questions about the difficult bits. Or we will make platitudinous and/or coercive remarks about how 'powerful' or 'vivid' or 'immediate' the poem is. This at least is the kind of teaching I used to do'.

Now this last bit really confused me Chris. Does it mean there was an even earlier Chris Woodhead, a sort of *Woodheadus* erectus, who was a traditionalist, and who then, somewhere along the long road to Damascus, became a bit of a liberal, *Woodheadus neanderthalensis*, before finally becoming traditional again, *Woodheadus sapiens?* There could be material for a whole set of *Dr Who* adventures here – Wood meets Chris, Chris meets Wood, Chris and Wood meet Head.

In this *TES* article Wood wrote: 'One fundamental reason (for not allowing a period of silence) is that we are deeply anxious that the children will take advantage of us and escape our control. Unless we crack the pedagogic whip we fear the circus animals will desert' ... "Tell us the answer sir, you know what it is'. To reply that you do not, and that your answer may be theirs, is likely to cause no little upset'. Well put, Mr Chrishead.

So there are many effective ways of teaching, and that is why most teachers use a mixture of approaches. Merely to attack 'progressives' or 'traditionalists' is too crude. Wood Chrishead seems to be talking good sense. I only hope Chris Woodhead will tolerate him.

Times Educational Supplement 17.2.95

A brush with a virtually clean sweep

There are exciting developments afoot in the inspection world. According to a thick yellow pamphlet from the Office for Standards in Education about the inspection of teacher training, the new buzz word is 'sweep'. Apparently inspectors will brush rapidly through the nation's teacher training courses doing 'sweep' inspections.

I think such speedy instant audits used to be called 'dipsticks' (the inspections that is, not the inspectors). In my innocence I always assumed that the word 'sweep' referred to the harmless act of cleaning up with a brush, but it obviously confirms the fact that inspection nowadays is becoming as daft as one. A huge PhD could be written on the industrial and commercial metaphors in education that Government agencies use in their papers.

As we deliver the curriculum in a cost-effective way to children (or emergent learning receptacles as I prefer to call them), inspectors sweep the nation, doing dipsticks, which involve calibrating teachers' performance indicators against national norms. In this anachronistic 19th century world of humming conveyor belts, oily machines manufacture a mass of identical commodities for a teeming peasantry. It is amazing, at the end of the production line on a Friday afternoon, that teachers still have enough oil left on their dipsticks to teach Year 3 Turbo or Year 9 Sump.

Sweep inspections are going to be the order of the day for teacher training, it says in the latest OFSTED missive. This news has left the nation agog with just one burning question. Sweep inspections are all very well, but will Sooty be coming too? After all, Sweep without Sooty would be like Laurel without Hardy. If I were Sweep I would make it clear to OFSTED – no Sooty, no Sweep. In this world of high comedy, it is only right that teacher-as-machine should be vetted by inspector-as-puppet.

Even more startling is the infotech nightmare of the future. As the 21st century dawns and the Information Superhighway unrolls, some zealots are planning the next wheeze – 'virtual' inspections. Just as you can put on a special helmet and sample 'virtual reality', that is a simulated three-dimensional computerised world in which you can zap space creatures, so too inspectors would not need to visit the real world of education.

Virtual reality offers numerous possibilities. Images are projected on to a screen inside the helmet, so it is already being used to train surgeons. There was even a virtual reality wedding in California, which may well end up one day in a virtual reality divorce. In future, inspectors would do 'virtual' inspections by simply calling up, through the internet, an institution's database. They could then read the relevant details of courses, staff qualifications, examination results, questionnaire responses, on their monitor, before you even had time to say, 'Get your thieving hands off our database, you virtual bastards'.

Yet there is nothing very 'futuristic' about the virtual reality model of inspection. The assumptions and values are the very same as the 19th century sweat shop model, only dressed up in 21st century artefacts. Children are cans of beans, teachers are operatives. The principal aim is to maximise beans output. So take off the overalls, wipe off the oil stains. Put on the white coat and sit at the keyboard and screen instead. Clinical.

However, we mustn't be spoilsports, so let's get excited at this 'virtual' caper. Just think of the possibilities, once it is accepted that education can be evaluated without actually soiling your hands on a visit. Nobody ever need leave their front room. Charts, figures and tables could whiz down the fibre optic cables at the speed of light. In case these raw numbers are thought to be too crude, then closed-circuit television could be used to show Mr Ramsbottom trying to teach music to 9 Sump with five pupils astride his chest. Mrs Hardcastle, ostensibly on sick leave with a bout of flu, could be viewed supervising the furniture van unloading her new carpet.

Ultimately, of course, the whole of education could go 'virtual'. Teachers would fax their lesson notes to the school. Pupils could stay at home and log in to the central information system. The virtual secretary would deal with awkward virtual parents by unplugging their virtual reality helmets. The virtual school nurse would only have to stick her dipstick into the computer system to make sure it was running, and insert the software equivalent of an aspirin if it wasn't. The virtual caretaker wouldn't even have to come in to clean up the virtual sick. We have ministers who are holograms, so why not go the whole hog?

To help Mr Dipstick, the lay inspector, the visual images could all be shown in simple cartoon form, with sub-titles for the slower learner. Mr Dipstick would make himself comfortable in his bath chair, open a box of dark chocolates, put on his virtual reality helmet, and watch Tom (the deputy head) chase Jerry (the disorganised teacher) down the corridor trying to get his end-of-term teacher assessments off him. Tom and Jerry would crash into Spike (the head), who would bark like mad (well, many heads are barking nowadays) and chase them both in the opposite direction. I told you virtual reality could be amazingly realistic.

At the end of the whole process Spike, the head, would step on a 'speak your weight' machine, arms laden with test scores, parent opinion questionnaires and truancy figures. A distant cracked voice would pronounce 'Below the national average – you have virtually failed – the virtual hit squad arrives next Thursday'. A few days later Sooty and Sweep would arrive wearing a couple of virtual reality helmets, ready to run the school. It could all happen. We have the technology. And some idiots have the will.

'Now stop being silly, Sweep', as Harry Corbett used to say.

Times Educational Supplement 26.5.95

Running, chasing, dodging, avoiding

You cannot keep sport and physical education out of the news about schools nowadays. It is not just league tables and other sporting analogies. John Major, no less, said a couple of weeks ago, 'Sport is fun .... fun, fun, fun'.

But then, it was the same 'fun, fun, fun' Major who announced his educational blueprint for the 21st century: 'I want children to learn to read, write and add up'. That was the entire vision. Blink and you missed it. He certainly has a way with English, when in full flow. The language that begat Shakespeare also begat Mr Monosyllable.

As a sports nut myself I am delighted to see sport and PE at the centre of the curriculum. British teachers are now Olympic gold medallists at some events – throwing the box file, putting the SAT, tossing the national curriculum folder. There was nothing special about Rob Andrew's 40 yard drop kick that beat Australia in the rugby World Cup. We have teachers who can kick an out-of-date national curriculum folder into a wastepaper basket from 50 yards, and with their back to it.

If Linford Christie packs up international sprinting, there is absolutely no problem. Just paint the running track to look like a school drive. Then shout in a loud voice 'Mrs Hardcastle has phoned in sick, is anybody free after assembly?', and twenty teachers will break seven seconds for the 100 metres

The sport-and-education metaphor came up again with the sad news of a dramatic rise in the numbers of head teachers suspended by their governors. The National Association of Head Teachers complained that heads were treated like football managers. Slip down the league table and the head is fired.

How long before heads are interviewed in television sports programmes? 'I was gutted, Brian. We've been taking each Ofsted as it comes, but it's hard to score against packed defences. The chairman assured me only last week that my job was safe, but then I read in the papers that he wants Ron Atkinson'.

If you look carefully at the PE national curriculum document, you can see the Government's master plan. Education is actually one big PE course. Take Key Stage 1, for example. The PE document states that pupils should be taught 'running, chasing, dodging, avoiding'. That sums up the behaviour of ministers in a nutshell.

Then there is Key Stage 2 with its 'challenges of a physical and problem-solving nature, eg negotiating obstacle courses'. This is obviously a reference to being a teacher. In the 'swimming' section, there is a coded Government tip for teachers on how to get to the front of the queue for a performance-related pay award. Just demonstrate 'a variety of means of propulsion using either arms or legs or both'.

It is in Key Stages 3 and 4 that the crucial Government advice for teachers is to be found. Right at the top of the PE programme it says 'How to prepare for particular activities and recover afterwards', which one half expects to recommend stiff vodkas before and after inspections and national tests.

The best hints for head teachers are also to be found in the 'swimming' section. Dealing with disgruntled teachers is covered by the requirement for 'two recognised strokes, one on the front and on the back', while the sections on 'personal survival' and 'rescue and resuscitation' duly recognise the strains of headship. 'Synchronised swimming' is clearly for crawlers who always pretend they are of one mind with their chairman of governors.

There are even more opportunities for sport to inform and influence the world of teaching and learning. Some schools already have a football 'yellow card' system for pupil discipline. Misbehave after a warning and you get a yellow card. Two yellow cards and your parents are brought in.

Inspectors could also use the cards held up by ice-skating judges. At the end of a lesson, up leaps the Russian judge (the registered inspector) with '5.1 for technical merit and 4.9 for artistic impression'. Boos and hisses from the class for the inspector. Large bunches of flowers thrown on to the floor for the teacher, who weeps and is consoled by his coach (the school secretary).

Cricket might have a role to play here as well. Two Ofsted inspectors could sit in school assembly at each end of the hall. When assembly is finished, one inspector leaps up and shout 'Owzthat!' in a loud voice. If the assembly is illegal, and it usually is, then the other inspector stands up and solemnly raises a finger to signal that the deputy head is 'out', his cracked solo rendition of the Beatles song 'Strawberry Fields For Ever' not being deemed to be a fair substitute for 'Onward Christian Soldiers'.

My favourite physical education story at the moment is about the PE teacher who locked two inspectors from the Office for Standards in Education in the changing room. She was concerned that Ofsted inspectors were snooping around unannounced all over the place, so she decided to lock up the changing room so they couldn't get in it. Unbeknown to her they were already inside, so she unwittingly locked them in. The pupils in the school had been told to be really friendly to the inspectors, so when they saw these two reluctant prisoners at the window, frantically waving to be let out, they cheerfully waved back.

Schools have developed many different tactics for coping with inspectors, but locking them away is a brilliant new strategy. It was the most hilarious response to school inspection since the teacher who took a photograph of an Ofsted inspector fast asleep in his lesson. As a way of funding sporting activities, schools could run a 'Lock up Ofsted week' to raise cash (Pay a tenner into school funds, or we won't let you out).

'Fun, fun, fun', as our Prime Minister so eloquently put it.

Times Educational Supplement 23.6.95

Nice little earner for the spiv inspector

Education usually has less than its share of dirty business. But naughty things have happened lately, so I have instituted the 'Arthur Daley Awards' for shabby practice in education. The much coveted 'Ada' will recognise supreme achievement in this highly specialised field.

The first prestigious Ada is awarded to those inspectors of the Office for Standards in Education to whom this astonishing warning was addressed in the 14th issue of the OFSTED Update for school inspection:

Conduct of Inspectors

'Several schools have brought to our attention situations where inspectors were thought to be misusing their position in order to seek work in a consultancy capacity. Although such concerns can arise as a result of genuine misinterpretation of good intentions, we want to draw the dangers specifically to the attention of inspectors.

'Guidance on the Code of Conduct states that inspectors should refrain from using their position to secure further employment for themselves, or others, where this would prejudice, or appear to prejudice, their impartiality or impair the integrity of an inspection. In particular the handing out of business cards has resulted in a number of complaints.

'We also advise that where inspectors offer 'free' advice following an inspection, the limits of what is being offered should be made clear and this should not be a prelude to seeking further paid work on the back of an inspection'.

These three paragraphs from OFSTED blew my mind. Since the privatisation of inspections, Her Majesty's Inspectorate has been turning in its collective grave. What on earth did it say on the business cards that these entrepreneurial inspectors handed out during inspections? 'Illegal assemblies? Call Holierthanthou Plc for expert advice'? 'Sid Spiv, Consultant Extraordinary'?

The last paragraph baffled me. How did 'free' advice become chargeable? Did these slimy inspectors, all smiles and affability, cheerfully offer a few tips and then send a bill later, or turn up round the back with an unmarked van and a cash register? If you've got an OFSTED coming up, keep a lookout for Sid Spiv.

Presumably de-briefing after an inspection nowadays goes like this: 'So to sum up, ladies and gentlemen, Swineshire School is below the national average in mathematics. Now we have some really nice maths tests available, only fifty quid a dozen. No, look, I like your face. To you, forty quid. All right, cor blimey, the missus'll kill me for this. Thirty quid, that's my final offer. Tell you what, I've gone completely crackers, it must be your bleedin' birthday today. Twenty quid – and an OFSTED T-shirt'. I can't remember this happening back in the days of HMI.

While Sid Spiv was avidly plying his seedy trade in the inspection business, the second Ada was being won comfortably by the Department for Education.

In the 21st century, researchers into media management will find rich pickings in the press releases from the Department for Education, or the 'Ministry of Truth' as it will be known. DFE press releases stretch the word 'truth' into hyperspace. Their main purpose is to persuade journalists, and the public, that all is well with Government policy.

A report comes out saying 'Government policy is about as effective as an aerosol at the North Pole'. Next day the DFE press release, under the headline 'Report supports Government education policy', states boldly, 'Mr Henry Farnes-Barnes, Minister of Truth, welcomed the Youmustbekidding Report, saying, 'This glowing report is a great testimony to the success of our North Pole fly spray policy for raising educational standards in inner cities'.'

Two years ago the National Commission on Education published a thorough report on the state of education. Last month it brought out an update on what had and had not been done by the Government. The Commission's own press release was headlined 'Education Commission signs off on note of dismay – 'Action has lagged behind rhetoric''. It went on to talk about a 'long catalogue of neglect'.

By contrast the DFE press release dismissed these criticisms as 'misplaced'. It documented examples of Government 'progress' it claimed had been ignored by the Commission. This 'progress' included 'education will be at the top of the Government's expenditure priorities as the economy delivers further growth' and various other meaningless events in an unspecified future. If that is 'progress', then I'm a banana, as the editor of *Private Eye* once said. Congratulations on your Ada, DFE. Arthur Daley himself takes his hat off to you. Even Sid Spiv, the bent inspector, is looking envious.

The third Ada goes to those naughty schools who are said to have cheated in the national tests. I don't know whether they were being egged on by Sid Spiv, but giving pupils the answers to the tests is definitely offside. It reminded me of a story told by one of our leading educational psychologists.

One day he went to a school to test children's reading. One pupil was tongue-tied. So the psychologist thought that, before he actually gave the boy the reading test, he ought to break the ice, engage in a bit of light conversation. However, there was only silence from the lad. The psychologist tried everything, conversation, banter, easy everyday questions. Not a sausage. Not one word crossed the boy's lips. The psychologist despaired. How could he do a reading test with a pupil who would not even open his mouth.

As a last resort, bringing all his years of experience to bear, he tried one desperate ruse. Isn't there anything you'd like to say to me before we start?', he asked, 'Anything at all?'. The lad furrowed his brow. With one enormous effort he slowly uttered seven words: 'Sit – card – duck – push – cow – hat – sheep'.

They were the first seven words of the psychologist's reading test. The boy's teacher had been coaching him in it all week.

Times Educational Supplement 7.7.95

The scratch-card guide to evaluation

Are you doing anything next Wednesday? At a bit of a loose end by any chance? Likely to spend the day kicking your heels, or playing patience, just to pass the time?

Well worry no more about how fill those empty hours. Get yourself down to the Copthorne Tara Hotel in London where, according to the information sheet I have been sent, you can spend the day at a conference entitled 'Making the Most of the National Lottery as a Funding Source'. Then, like Eton and other deserving institutions have done, you might land a bit of lottery loot.

Among several speakers you will hear during this exciting opportunity to learn about lottery funding is one Virginia Bottomley MP. In a letter reproduced in the programme, she writes: 'I will be giving the Government's view on how the Lottery has developed as a funding source and how we see it stimulating wider participation and interest in sport, the arts and the nation's heritage throughout the United Kingdom. I welcome this event as a very useful forum for all those involved, or interested in, Lottery funding'.

Can't wait to book your place? Well the bad news is that, if you want to hear Virginia's pearls of wisdom, you had better write a cheque for up to £411.25, because that is what it will cost you to attend the day conference, though it is less for charities. This does include what is quaintly called 'luncheon', a somewhat dated term for, I hope, at the top price, half a ton of caviar washed down with a dozen bottles of Bollinger. You will probably need the champagne to recover from the shock of having parted with up to 400-plus smackers for the privilege of listening to Virginia bloody Bottomley. She should pay us to turn up.

In this scratchcard society, those that have little money are persuaded to part with some of it in the faint hope that they might get lucky. It may be just a bit of fun for those who can afford it, but a lottery raises much of its cash from the desperate. It is a squalid way of funding what should be public services.

All of which is a roundabout way of saying that life itself is a bit of lottery nowadays, especially when it comes to the assessment of teaching ability. I was intrigued at the irony of the account in the *Times Educational Supplement* 'Diary' column two or three weeks ago about Senior Chief Inspector Chris Woodhead being assessed by HMI for talks he gave to them at their annual in-house OFSTED conference.

For those who missed the Diary piece, what happened was as follows: HMI have to evaluate speakers at their conference, using the same five point scale they employ on their visits to classrooms. Chris 'Name-the-Bad-Teachers' Woodhead was given a clutch of the two lowest grades, 4s and 5s, on such features as 'usefulness', 'interest' and 'presentation skills'. So far, very ironic, ha ha. Poor old Chris fails his OFSTED and has to come up with an action plan. Tough toenails, no excuses, it's a hard world, on your bike.

There is, however, a serious side to all this. What was striking about the evaluations was that, although large numbers of HMI gave him the bottom grades, some marked him higher. For example, the spread of marks on the criterion 'interest' was very wide, with 11% giving him the top category, grade 1. A further 25% ticked grade 2, 28% grade 3 and 36% awarded the bottom grades 4 and 5. On 'presentation skills' no-one gave him the top grade, but 51% ticked grades 2 and 3, while 49% awarded grades 4 and 5.

My reaction to this was quite simple. Don't stand around. Dial 999. Ask for all the emergency services – police, ambulance, fire brigade, Virginia Bottomley, the lot. If Inspector A gives grade 1 for the same performance that Inspector B rates a grade 5, then this must be national crisis time.

It confirms what many of us have argued for years, which is that the assessment of teaching is a highly subjective matter, and that OFSTED can be a bit of a lottery. One man's meat is another man's hit squad. Think of all the teachers being inspected at this very moment who might get a grade 5 from Harry Hardcheese, but would perhaps have earned a grade 1 from Simon Softee.

This whole saga illustrates beautifully the problems of assessing teaching. I don't always agree with his message, but I think that old Wooders is actually a good speaker, so I might want to give him grade 4 for 'content', but grade 1 for 'presentation skills'. Someone else might agree with every word he says and award grade 1 for 'content'.

It is, however, all too easy to allow our emotional reactions to 'content' or 'personal appearance' to colour our appraisal of general 'teaching skill'. Different aspects of teaching sometimes need to be kept separate from one another. I hope Wooders learns from his own experience at the hands of his assessors and recognises that the evaluation of human ability is not always a simple open-and-shut matter.

So I have devised my totally impartial British Instruction Assessment Scale (BIAS) for the completely objective award of a grade 1 for teaching. Superteachers must manifest the following characteristics:

- Wear elbow patches and Hush Puppies
- Say 'Ey up' when a pupil misbehaves
- Like Yorkshire Pudding
- Not have nodding dogs on the rear shelf of their car
- Support Sheffield Wednesday
- Hate Arsenal

Copies of the BIAS scale are available from Virginia Bottomley for £411.25 (including luncheon and scratchcard).

Times Educational Supplement 3.11.95

A parallel universe in paper, my Dears

One of the best features of a new year is throwing things away. Weeding bookshelves of documents no longer needed, nowadays known as a 'Dearing', is more pleasurable than cleaning a full blackboard or emptying rubbish out of the car. After a hard year's work, there's nothing to beat a good Dearing. I have just put half a decade of mad curriculum disease into the shredder. It brought back a few memories.

The 1989 science curriculum had electricity and magnetism as Attainment Target 11. In May 1991 a new proposal for five Attainment Targets instead of seventeen appeared. Good old electricity and magnetism were now in Attainment Target 5, 'Forces'. Four months later, in September 1991, another green bottle fell off the wall, and there were only four topics. Electricity and magnetism survived, in new Attainment Target 4, 'Physical Processes'. 'Looby dooby doo, I'm a petunia', sang the nation's teachers in unison.

The national curriculum baffled scientists by generating its own electricity and magnetism, propelling itself into and out of Attainment Target 97b 'Scrymzzical Breeglebums', or 36m(iii), 'Flangical Triceps', completely defying the laws of conventional physics. There were no tears shed as that particular load of drivel went into the waste bin, I can tell you, though I kept a few souvenirs for days when a little mirth may be needed.

I was in mid-Dearing when the phone rang. 'Hello', said a voice, 'It's ABC Market Research here. My name's Denzil. We're doing a report for the Office for Standards in Education on the use that people in education are making of OFSTED documents'. I hesitated. Was this a wind-up? Was it some friend who had finally flipped and started playing practical jokes? Was it chance that had brought together the ritual shredding of one set of daft documents with an inquisition about another? And if it was indeed true, would anyone ever believe me if I told them about it?

It was genuine. Denzil, a very nice man, really was doing a piece of market research on the use that people in education are making of

OFSTED documents. It is known as 'cold calling'. Market researchers ring you up and conduct a telephone interview. They then sit there with a set of checklists on their knee, trying to squeeze you into one of three or four crude stereotyped categories – more or less what OFSTED itself does to schools, if you think about it. The giveaway comes when they utter statements like, 'So would you say that you are 'fairly happy' or 'very happy' about the quality of British bootlaces then?'.

Anyway, Denzil set off on his trek: 'What is the main use you make of OFSTED documents?'. I looked across at the near 500 page ring-bound file on how to inspect a school. It had certainly come in handy propping open the door when shifting obsolete national curriculum documents out to the skip, but presumably Denzil's pen was poised over categories such as 'information', or 'staff development', rather than 'door stop'.

I thought hard. 'Do you want an honest answer?'. 'Yes, of course'. 'Well, the answer is that I do use it for in-service courses, but my main use is 'satire''.

There was a pause. 'I beg your pardon?'. 'Satire. I satirise it. It's been a godsend. It's very thorough, but it's frightened everybody witless. Teachers need a laugh on a dark December evening, so I take the piss out of it'. Long pause while Denzil hunts through his categories.

As Denzil ploughed methodically on with his questions, the parallels between the national curriculum in its first manifestation, and OFSTED in its present incarnation, became increasingly marked in my mind. Both generated too much paper, most of it unread by many teachers. Both were founded on lack of faith, on the identical suspicion – that teachers could not be trusted to do a decent job and needed a heavy, blunt, bureaucratic instrument, reinforced by cumbersome statutory authority, to cudgel them into shape. Both caused great anxiety, and wasted hours of the time of busy people.

Many teachers have not yet been Ofstedded (new past participle). The process is only rescued by the presence, for the time being, of a few real inspectors who know (a) what they are doing and (b) how to hide their lay inspector in the nearest lockable cupboard.

If more teachers had been Ofstood (pluperfect subjunctive passive), they would have seen what it is like – the mass of preliminary information needed, much of it unnecessary; the disruption to the school's working life; the Lord Mayor's Show; the gibberish of the final report; the feeling of having been done over, however skilfully; the lack of follow-up, continuity and after-care.

One of the saddest features of OFSTED is when bewildered hard-working staff, in a tough downtown area, read the mechanical prose of the final report, with its emphasis on their exam results being below the national average. Huge prominence, in the recommendations of OFSTED reports, is given to structures: the school's development plan, management and administration, whether it has a legal assembly. There are too few recommendations on relationships, classroom process, imagination, content, commitment, expectation, community, the very lifeblood of successful education. This is not surprising. The process has been privatised. It had to be designed so that any dickhead could administer it.

Denzil was on to his last question. 'Is there anything else you want to say about OFSTED?'. Sorry, Denzil, there isn't time. Let us just hope that the 'averagely satisfactory' and 'satisfactorily average' language and culture of present-day OFSTED will one day be gleefully shredded. We need a far better system of quality assurance, with much more attention to improving what happens in the classroom, as well as support and follow-up for schools that have been inspected. Real and lasting development for the better is more important than neat bureaucratic categorisation. January 1996 for a good Dearing?

Times Educational Supplement 6.1.95

A masterpiece of coded codswallop

'To market, to market, to buy a fat pig. Home again, home again, jiggety jig. To market, to market, to buy a fat hog. Home again, home again, jiggety jog'. This traditional nursery rhyme is a simple tale about buying and selling in the market. They don't write them like that any more.

Well, they do, actually. If you want to read a late 20th century story about buying and selling in the market that lacks the innocent charm of the fat pig nursery rhyme, then just feast your eyes on this dazzling gem. I shall leave you to guess the context, but the first clue is that it is a letter.

The letter is about tendering arrangements and it begins 'Dear Contractor'. Any ideas so far? An invitation to Wimpey and Tarmac to bid for a new supermarket perhaps? Not even warm. Read on. I shall delete the giveaway phrases.

'As you may know, we recently invited the market to supply ....., using competitive tendering'. Any clearer? A delivery of widgets? A lorry load of spigots? A few thousand litres of snake oil? No, still miles away. Try a bit more. In fact try a lot more.

'There was an encouraging response from Contractors, but we still have a shortfall'. (Surely it must be widgets. They can get terribly scarce at this time of year. No, sorry, have another go). 'We ... intend to contract directly ... We have fixed a 'rate for the job', which delivers value for money, which is attractive ... but which will not disadvantage contractors seeking team members for ....' (All right, teams of snake oil vendors then. It must be. Not quite, but you are getting warmer). 'I hope this letter explains why we have had to take these steps for ...., and how we intend to manage the process so that the market is not disadvantaged'.

Give in? Right, I will tell you. It has nothing to do with spigots, ball bearings, catering size cans of baked beans, or alternative supplies of gas. It describes the arrangements for school inspections, and it comes from the Office for Standards in Education, so in a way it is about alternative supplies of gas. It sees the world of education not as one inhabited by human beings, but as a market, full of contractors and tenders, grasping whatever loot they can wrest. Bring back the fat pig, jiggety jig. At least it rhymed.

This is only one of four peerless masterpieces about the school inspection market which I have read recently. A second gem from the tireless OFSTED fount describes a set of three digit codes, each of which gives unsuccessful contractors (Oops! Slipping into the market jargon) some information about why their tender for a school inspection was rejected. I swear I am making none of this up, by the way. So 365, for example, means 'beaten on price', while 366 stands for 'well beaten on price'. Presumably 399 indicates 'absolutely pasted on price, and members of your team smell'.

Intriguing codes include 342, 'lay inspector(s) over/underloaded' (was their rucksack too heavy/light?), and 309 'tender included subjects outside the scope of the inspection'. In this last case, presumably the contractor wrote, 'We are particularly looking forward to inspecting the mediaeval cosmology and Sanskrit translation courses in this infant school'.

A third superlative missive from the OFSTED factory describes the quality control of registered inspectors. The interesting section reads: 'We will cease grading Registered Inspectors. It will be incumbent on us to report on their fitness and competence to remain on the register, but that does not require a five-point grading system'.

Oh really? Could this letter be from the same OFSTED whose chief inspector Chris Woodhead has just sent out the fourth of the market masterpieces to come my way? This is the letter to headteachers explaining about the reporting on 'very good and very poor teachers'. Old Wooders is requiring these very same inspectors, who apparently do not themselves require a five-point grading system, to report to the head any teacher who gets a grade 1 or 2, or a grade 6 or 7. According to Wooders this will provide the head 'with valuable management information'.

Read the shabby, ill-conceived letter about reporting good and poor teachers if you missed it. On as little as two lessons a teacher could be labelled 'good' or 'bad'. The teacher can complain about the inspector's conduct to OFSTED, but not about the professional judgment of inspectors. So you can write in if he breaks wind in mid-lesson, but not if he can't tell a squirrel from a hippopotamus.

If the inspector turns out to be a wally, then you may only complain to the head. You can offer the inspector 'exceptional personal reasons' which may have contributed to the quality of the lesson. So you can mention your ailing granny and ingrown toenail, but not point out that the inspector may be a prat.

In theory that sounds fine. After all, OFSTED reports on individuals are only advisory, it is said. But four years later, when OFSTED inspectors return, they will, of course, ask the head what has been done about those 'bad' teachers, however frail the evidence at the time.

I can foresee nothing but trouble. The right-wing may feel that this is the way to rumble poor teachers. Would that it were. Wait until some traditionalist is given a grade 7 by a trendy inspector for spending too much time on spelling, and the system will not seem quite so apt. Anyone who knows anything about research into classroom skills can forecast what will happen. The lawyers must be rubbing their hands. Bags I the prosecution brief when inspectors are sued for inadequate judgments.

To market, to market, to fail a bad lad. Home again, home again, OFSTED's gone mad.

Times Educational Supplement 19.4.96

And the greatest of these is clarity

I have been desperately looking for a bit of clarity. In the confused and confusing world in which we live, a clear analysis is like an oasis, a refuge from the wilderness that surrounds it. How can education be improved? Are standards going up, down, or in circles? Are teachers a gang of wild trendies? Is Woodhead a Klingon? 'More light' as Goethe said, just before he snuffed it.

There is not much clarity about whether we do better or worse than other countries. It depends what you look at. Most international comparisons tend to be based on maths tests. There are comparisons in other subjects, but they are harder to do, as everyone has a different history or science syllabus. But then, the same applies to maths. Our maths coverage tends to be wider than is the case in many other countries, so the kind of maths test given by the researchers is crucial. We usually do very badly at 'number', but not so poorly in 'geometry'.

You can gain a bit of clarity by observing classrooms at first hand in other countries. The German system is often praised uncritically, yet I have seen some brain corrodingly ineffective teaching in German schools. On the other hand German vocational education is very impressive, and many teachers are good at getting high standards of work out of lower ability children.

In the so-called 'Pacific Rim', I have seen lessons where the level of industry was formidable, but where there was not one jot of appeal to children's imagination. Small wonder that some of these countries are now keen on 'individualism', realising that endless copying does not produce an inspired adult. If there were an international league table for 'imagination' I would expect us to be very high in it. We are the inventing capital of the world, but are useless at exploiting our imagination.

I was very interested in the study of education in Taiwan reported in the TES a couple of weeks ago. Taiwanese children do better than us at maths, so what was their secret?

Apparently teachers and pupils are encouraged to go to sleep for half an hour during the school day. I have occasionally felt drowsy while watching someone else's lesson, but never actually nodded off in one of my own, so that could be an interesting experience.

We were also told that Taiwanese teachers enjoy high status. Yet they have complained at having to collect urine samples. Could this be related to higher pupil achievement? British teachers have low status in the eyes of politicians, and they are more used to being peed on than actually collecting the stuff, but I was not clear why Taiwanese teachers had to do it. Perhaps it was to do with dope testing. Talking about dopes, if the loony right-wing think tanks that advise the government hear of the idea, then compulsory tiddling into a flask will probably find its way into the next election manifesto.

Still in quest of greater clarity I came across the most wonderful attempt I have witnessed for many an age. Indeed, not since the demise of the School Examinations and Assessment Council has there been anything like it. But as one SEAC closes another OFSTED opens, and our special chums the Office for Standards in Education have brought the concept of 'clarification' to new interstellar heights.

You may well know that most heads and teachers have an uneasy feeling that their assembly is illegal and that they are responsible for personal, social and moral development, but are not always certain that what they are doing meets the 'official' requirements nowadays.

Dear old OFSTED, ever helpful, has issued a statement to help us all understand. So hold on to your hat, because anyone not fluent in advanced Klingon may find it a little difficult to follow. The beginning is promising and upbeat: 'Some confusion remains about the respective purposes and functions of Section 9 and Section 13 inspections in relation to religious education, collective worship and provision for pupils' spiritual, moral, social and cultural development'.

Yes yes, quite right, OFSTED, there is indeed some confusion, so clarify it for me. Go on, give it me straight. Get into top gear. Speak your wise words of clarification. Go for it. Hit me right there. I can take it.

'The provision of Section 13 of the 1992 Act (as amended by Section 259 of the 1993 Act) cover **denominational religious education** and **collective worship** in voluntary and other schools. The inspection of pupils' spiritual, moral, social and cultural development must be covered by the Section 9 inspection. However, Section 9 inspections must not cover denominational religious education or the content of collective worship where the latter falls to be inspected under Section 13.

'The strengths and weaknesses of the school's provision for the spiritual development of its pupils (*Schedule* section 5.3) and their response (*Schedule* section 4.2) should view spiritual development in the wider interpretation of the *Framework*. Pupils' spiritual, moral, social and cultural development may also be included in the section 13 report if the inspector decides to cover this'.

Er, come again, OFSTED. If that is clarification, then please confuse me again. Ah, what's this, there's more. Thank goodness.

'There will be further expansion of this guidance in the *Guide to the Law* Occasional Paper which will appear during the summer term'.

Phew what a relief! I can't wait. So that's it then. My quest for the ultimate clarification is over. We now know that the inspection of schools' splindongerous pongifiles and pupils' denunciated motorway cones must be dealt with under Segment 99.99 of the collective workshops mortality, and is thus clearly the responsibility of regimented introspectors doing a Segment at 9-13 a.m. Unless, of course, they decide otherwise.

Don't say you weren't told.

Times Educational Supplement 17.5.96

Tales of Baker daze and Sherpa Chris

So Mrs Thatcher got her ideas on education from her hairdresser, or possibly from her cleaner, according to the late great Kenneth Baker in an interview with Michael Barber reported in the TES a couple of weeks ago.

Apparently she would go into Cabinet meetings clutching what Baker called 'some rather tatty bit of paper which she had been sent by somebody, goodness knows who..... Sometimes this rogue briefing was spot on, other times it was completely mad'. I was left wondering, given the lunacy of those years, how Baker knew which was which.

It could explain a lot. Since the right-wing ideologues were supposed to be her main inspiration, did they double up as her hairdresser? After all, she usually had a rather bulbous lump of topiary on top of her head, so perhaps it was the handiwork of someone more at home with the thoughts of Adam Smith than with a pair of shears.

My mum used to be a cleaner, but she never got the chance to design the national curriculum. Mrs Thatcher's cleaner lived in Lambeth and, according to Baker, 'was worried that her children were going to be educated by a lot of Trots'. I wonder if, as she sprinkled the Vim on Mrs Thatcher's immaculate MFI sink unit, she was inspired to create those exciting SATs for seven year olds on floating and sinking, that had the nation's infant schools slopping knee deep in water and disgustingly sodden pineapples.

Or did Monsieur Pierre, as he chiselled the Great One's locks, dream up all those Attainment Targets? 'Tell you what'. Snip snip. 'How about seventeen ATs for science and fourteen for maths. A little more off the top?'. Snip snip. 'How's that for length? Or what about this one, this'll have you in stitches. Why not make teachers tick thousands of little boxes, so the Trots have no time to teach all that Marxist-Leninist theory? String 'em all up I say. A bit more mousse, madam?'.

Actually I must say I found it hard to read Baker's unique version of 1980s history without recourse to the airline sick bag I always have to hand on these occasions. There it was again, the story of the man who bravely battled on from triumph to triumph, never a false step. Any errors were down to someone else, like the teaching profession. So when Michael Barber described him as 'a minister of rare political talent' I have to admit that these were not words that leapt immediately into my mind. 'Complete' and 'Wally' got there first.

These profiles and images of public figures are always fascinating. In the many pen portraits of Chris Woodhead there is always the mention of his interest in mountaineering. Fearless Wooders intimates that he likes a scrap and will take on anybody or anything, regardless of danger – Everest, the Matterhorn, Mrs Fothergill who teaches Year 2.

There he was again on *Panorama* last week telling teachers to spend 60% of their maths lessons teaching the whole class. I didn't think he went far enough. What about the remaining 40%? My own suggestion would be 39% for copying off the blackboard and one per cent for scratching your bum.

This latest attack on trendy teachers was sparked off because Wooders was impressed by children in other countries getting better test scores than our pupils. As a believer in the validity of exam results he would presumably have no time for the woolly 1980s progressive who criticised traditional English teachers, called examinations 'pernicious' and wrote: 'An even more intransigent problem is that of measuring the progress of any individual child. For what criteria does the orthodoxy offer the classroom teacher to help him evaluate this progress?'.

But hold on a minute. The author of this coruscating attack on examinations and traditional English teachers was none other than Sherpa Woodhead himself. Back in the 1980s, shortly before the Baker era, good old Chris got on his mountaineering gear and had a real go at English 'traddies' in a journal article I came across. Just listen to this.

'It is not really surprising that in practice the majority of them (English teachers) abandon the theory which they encountered in training or on in-service courses in favour of a more mundane concentration on the extent to which children can spot the simile or remember the story line. Intellectually mundane such practices may be, but they do at least hold the chance of professional satisfaction: a teacher can feel he has taught something'.

'It is factors like these and not the shadow of public examinations, pernicious as the influence of examinations certainly is, that largely inhibit English teachers from developing English lessons in a way which utilises theory. As I have said, teachers who are conscious of this failure and are prepared to admit it frequently explain it by arguing that their teaching is distorted from its true purposes by the demands of the examination syllabuses. But ultimately that ludicrous insistence which characterises so many literature examinations, an insistence on memorised fact and on techniques of practical criticism wholly inappropriate to the intelligence and maturity of most candidates, is a symptom rather than a cause'.

I would quote more, but we traditionalists find it far too progressive, so read for yourself 'Dream and Waking: Theory and Practice in the Teaching of Literature' in the journal *Use of English*, volume 33.2, pages 3 to 15.

So the vital question remains: what would the fearless Sherpa say if Donald Duck became Prime Minister tomorrow? To which the answer is, 'Quack quack'. More or less what he says now, and said then, come to think of it.

Times Educational Supplement 14.6.96

Fear and loathing in Scabville

Picture the scene. Little Piddlington Primary School is in the middle of an OFSTED inspection. Elspeth Scattergood, assiduous Year 3 teacher, is being quizzed by zealous inspector Ivor Checklist, fully badged (one week in the Cosa Nostra Hotel, Southport), pen and clipboard quivering. The conversation goes like this:

Ivor Checklist	Have you got a book cupboard?
Elspeth Scattergood	Er, we keep... I, er, like the books out in the room, where....
IC	Have you got a book cupboard?
ES	Well, you see, there are some books over there, and I, er....
IC	Have you got a book cupboard?
ES	Well, no, er...not as such, I er...

Ivor Checklist puts a cross in his 'Has/has not got a book cupboard' tick box.

The conversation sums up what is happening in primary schools nowadays when the inspector calls. It is like an arcade game in which the Programmed meet the Bewildered. The good side of it all is that there is now, in theory at least, a regular pattern of inspection and the procedures being used are published, albeit in 493 pages of somewhat forbidding text. There are, however, far more problems than benefits.

First of all the very process strikes fear into the hearts of heads and teachers. Forget prunes, figs, bran flakes and laxatives. Primary heads never go to the doctor nowadays if they are constipated. They just get a colleague to whisper, 'OFSTED are coming', and the medical problem is cured instantly. The reason for the stark terror is not merely the thought of being inspected. That can often turn out to be a positive experience. It is partly, despite the enormous handbook, anxiety about the unknown, and partly the mechanical nature of the exercise.

If you are busting a gut in difficult circumstances in a downtown school, then knowing that some prominence will be given, in the

'Standards and quality' section near the beginning of the report, to the statement 'The standards in English and mathematics are well below the national average', is a killer blow which no amount of subsequent disarming will mitigate. Hello front page of the *Scabville Gazette*.

Once the inspection exercise was privatised much of what followed was predictable. If, as Kenneth Clarke said, anyone can inspect a school, even a butcher, then the procedures must be conceived so that they can be consistently applied. That is the rationale for the minutely detailed handbook and the tick sheet approach. Hence the ludicrous amount of preparatory work that schools put in before the fateful knock at the door.

Of course, in retrospect, some teachers say that the process was not as bad as they had feared. The whole exercise is partly rescued by the presence, for the time being, of several former HMI and LEA inspectors who are able to bend what less experienced inspectors would regard as an inflexible framework.

Nor is it surprising that OFSTED is having great difficulty finding enough primary inspectors, especially for small schools. Inspection is now a business, so many, though not all, of those doing it are looking for a decent profit. Tramping off to a three teacher school in some moorland wilderness, with the dubious pleasure of a few nights at the Sheep Shearers' Arms in the company of a retired Technology adviser and a redundant snow shoveller, is not exactly an alluring commercial prospect.

Before long the whole process must be reviewed, to establish a sensible professional structure of local and national inspection and support. And Ivor Checklist should be pensioned off so that he can return to his former occupation as a speaking clock.

Times Educational Supplement 9.9.94

Chapter 3
The last Quango

JCB approach is GBH on the image

If there are a single biscuit left to be taken nowadays, then the latest Government wheeze takes it. Schools are in desperate need of repair, thousands of teachers may lose their jobs, there is not enough money for books and equipment. So what does the Government do? Dial 999? Build new schools? Set up a book fund? No, none of these.

The Government announces that it is appointing some additional supremo, to be called apparently the 'Chief Contractor', whose job it will be to improve teachers' image. In the derelict world of politics in which we now live, that is what we academics, after deep reflection on every philosophical standpoint from Plato to the present day, and profound analysis of all the relevant contextual features, call a barrel of crap.

Government strategy on education consists of creating a problem; then, against all advice, compounding it; next, accusing everyone else of starting it; before finally paying a fortune to resolve it. This is precisely what happened with the first version of the national curriculum: it was far too complex, everybody complained about it, ministers insisted on ploughing on to the end of the furrow, then they blamed the educational establishment, whoever they were, for the very muddle they themselves had put through Parliament, and finally they congratulated themselves for calling in Sir Ron Dearing to clear up the mess.

It all reminds me of a bizarre arsonists' convention. The arsonists meet, decide which building to torch, then they denounce the firebug, call the fire brigade and claim the reward. Teachers have a poor image largely because they have been rubbished in speeches and in the press by the very ministers whose successors are now having to hire image consultants to repair the damage. Very sick. It's enough to rot your elbow patches.

Image consultancy is a legacy of the Kenneth Baker era. Like the Ancient Mariner's albatross, the belief that the image of something is more important than its reality, continues to hang round the neck of education, nowadays in the form of glossy brochures and image consultants. As schools battle on against the odds, with teachers doing more and more for less and less, the mirage of Mr Smug lingers in the air. Look up as you walk through a school and you will see hanging there, like a wisp of cigar smoke, Baker's bespectacled smile, as his after image still pulls the invisible strings.

No doubt the Chief Contractor will now be paid a zillion a year, and for what? The very term 'Chief Contractor' suggests the usual market-mad approach. Presumably people will bid for the contract. Or does the word 'Contractor' imply that someone from the building trade will do it, using all the subtlety of the JCB approach to image making? 'Roll up, roll up, semi-detached teachers on the left, completely detached teachers on the right'.

More importantly, what will the Chief Contractor actually do? Will the conversation go something like this?

'Ah, come in Mr Ramsbottom – Albert, isn't it?'

'Er, yes, Chief Contractor, Albert Ramsbottom, I teach PE at Gasworks Council School'.

'Indeed, indeed. Now let's have a look at you, Albert. Yes, I can see some possibilities. Is that your Hillman Imp outside, by the way, the blue one with the yellow front door?'

'Yes, Chief Contractor, I'm sorry about the door, only somebody ran into me and I couldn't afford a new door, so I had to get a second hand one. I'll paint it blue as soon as I've got enough paint, but I can only afford one touch-up pencil a month on my salary'.

'Well, I was thinking more of a Jaguar XJS or a Mercedes 500 SL, something with a bit more image, but we'll leave that for the moment. Now look here, Albert, I'll get straight to the point. I'm not happy with your name. It sounds so, well, Northern'.

'But my dad was called Albert, and my grandad'.

'We need something a bit more up-market. How about changing it by deed poll to Algernon Cholmondley? Yes? Good, that's settled then, I like the ring of it. So the next matter, or 'image challenge' as I like to call it, is the name of your school. You see Algy, it's all wrong. 'Gasworks' sounds so common, 'Council' suggests you haven't had the good sense to opt out, and 'School' is much too ordinary'.

'But we're right next to the gasworks, Chief Contractor, and a lot of the pupils' parents work there'.

'No, it just won't do, Algy. I see it more as 'Harvard Executive College', so make sure you have a new sign erected at the entrance'.

'But we're in Scunthorpe, Chief Contractor'.

'No matter, research into image making shows that clients are willing to suspend disbelief. Now, we must do something about your track suit. Why does it say 'PE, Loughborough' on the back?'

'That's where I did my training. It's highly regarded in the PE world'.

'I'm sorry, Algy. I don't like the sound of the subject or the place, not enough oomph. So I want you in a gold shell suit with 'Aerobic Science, Oxford' on the back'.

'But I don't think they do PE at Oxford'.

'No matter. If you'd like to report next door before you leave, Algy, you'll be given the full manicure, hair tint and dental treatment. Our colour consultant will issue you with a personalised wardrobe brief, and I'm prescribing our twenty hour elocution course to get rid of some of your Northern vowels.

'Throw those Hush Puppies in the large dustbin by the door, and collect your designer shoes and signed photograph of Kenneth Baker as you leave. Now, anything else?'.

'Thank you, Chief Contractor, there is just one more thing. I hope you won't think I'm being greedy. But do you happen to have a spare pair of those Giorgio Armani elbow patches you're wearing?'.

Times Educational Supplement 3.3.95

The night Santa called it quits

It was Christmas Eve in Snowland. A light flurry of snow swept across the school yard. Santa Claus looked at his watch. Only the governors of Snowland School would dream of having their annual governors' meeting at eight o'clock on Christmas Eve. Why he had agreed to be Chairman of governors he would never know.

'Well, may we start?', he began, 'I've got to go on my round at midnight, and I promised Mrs Claus I'd drop in for a bite to eat before I set off'. The motley assortment of governors slowly abandoned their lukewarm tea and over-baked macaroons. 'They were a Technology project', the head said apologetically, as the better prepared governors discarded their curled up sandwiches and calcified cakes and reached for their Rennies. He glared daggers at Mr Oldfield, the Head of Technology, who was also a staff governor.

There was no love lost between Oldfield and the head. He saw the head as an oleaginous creep who smarmed round the governors to feather his own nest. The head in turn saw him as an unreconstructed woodwork teacher, whose vision of technology was a string cutter. 'Don't blame me squire', Oldfield muttered, 'I never wanted cookery in our bloody faculty anyway. It should have stayed in home economics where it belonged'.

'May we start then please?', Santa Claus repeated. The sociology of being a school governor had always baffled him. As an outsider he found himself at the centre of intrigues, manoeuvres and nuances he barely understood. 'Item 1', he began, 'Apologies. Do we have any apologies?'. There were none. Sadly that would mean he had to contend with Mrs Plant who fancied herself as an expert on constitutional law.

'Item 2. Minutes of our last meeting', he continued, 'May I sign these as a correct record?'.

'Mr Chairman'. Oh no, here it comes, Santa thought to himself as Mrs Plant launched her first fusillade. 'Are you going to take the OFSTED inspection under 'matters arising', or as a substantive item under 'Future issues' later?', she declaimed in that voice that had shattered a thousand icebergs. She sat back and beamed the smug look with which she always patronised the governors when she thought she had made a telling point.

'We'll take OFSTED later', Santa replied, his stomach beginning to protest at the indigestible cup cake he had foolishly consumed before the meeting. Outside the window something rustled. It was the reindeer getting restless as the snow thickened. There was Dancer and Prancer, the two lead reindeer, and Wally and Plonker, the two OFSTED inspectors, who graded all the chimneys as 'above', 'below' or 'at' the national average, and helped pull the 'generally satisfactory' sledge around the world.

'I wonder if we can move Item 12 up the agenda', the head oiled, 'It's an important item and I wouldn't want it neglected by coming late in the evening'. Small wonder. With his usual self-interest at heart, the little twerp was as transparent as ever. Item 12 was about performance-related bonuses for the head and deputies. There had never any difficulty casting the annual production of 'Snow White and the Seven Dwarfs' since he had been appointed. The part of Dopey cast itself.

Santa sighed. He really must have been mad to take on the chairmanship. 'Yes, we'll take it after your report', he said, 'In fact perhaps you could give us your report now'. The head preened himself. As ever this was the moment he had been waiting for and had dress rehearsed a hundred times.

There followed an intricately crafted fantasy that told of unparalleled achievement. In a nutshell, the school ran perfectly and the head was a resounding success. His teacher colleagues were invisible in this orgy of self-congratulation. Mr Oldfield's neck got redder as the saga unfolded. Unable to restrain himself, he burst in with 'I think the staff might just have made the odd contribution, Mr Chairman'. Santa nodded. 'Yes, of course'.

'Mr Chairman'. Mrs Plant's scalpel voice jerked Santa out of the somnolence into which he had sunk during the head's panegyric. 'May I ask if the school has fulfilled all the attainment targets and programmes of study of the statutory orders of the national curriculum?'. Mrs Plant sank back, swelling with pride, oblivious to the sheer meaninglessness of her question, which hit the meeting like a stun grenade. She had spent half an hour reading national curriculum documents to hand craft that one.

'I wonder if we could hold that most interesting and well conceived question, and just slide seamlessly into Item 12 now that I've concluded my report', the head cooed, 'You see, I think my report shows that I have met all the performance criteria for ......' 'What about the OFSTED report?', Mr Oldfield boomed. 'OFSTED report?', Santa asked, thrown by the head's deft footwork and Mr Oldfield's belligerence.

'Yes, the bloody OFSTED report', Oldfield repeated, 'Basically it said that the staff were running their socks off and that the school management left much to be desired'. The governors shuffled uncomfortably.

'I'm glad you mentioned that', Mrs Plant intoned. 'I've been looking at the OFSTED inspection handbook, and on page 56, paragraph three of the salmon coloured pages......'.

Santa Claus closed his eyes. As the glassware in the room shattered piece by piece at the intensity of Mrs Plant's torrent, his headache worsened. Why had he agreed to become chairman? Why did the head love himself so much? If he gave him his very best present, would even that make Mr Oldfield happy? Would the biggest sack on his sledge be an effective gag for Mrs Plant? Could he stand being chairman of governors any longer?

As the snow swirled ever more densely outside, he made his decision. Next year he would resign and concentrate on his annual trek round the world. At least that was manageable. And he could see an end to it.

Times Educational Supplement 23.12.94

Bombarded by reams of inanity

A thick envelope from the Department for Education has been arriving in several hundred schools recently. It is addressed to the Headteacher and it comes from something called the 'Efficiency Scrutiny Team'. It contains an enormous 30 page pack consisting of a covering letter and 52 items to complete. It is a questionnaire about – wait for it – the paperwork received by schools.

If there is one group experiencing the 'feelcrap' factor nowadays it is people in schools. To mail them yet more paperwork, this time about paperwork itself, is the ultimate sick joke. It is like sending somebody in the intensive care unit an entry form for the London marathon, or buying members of Alcoholics Anonymous a gallon of lager.

The questionnaire itself is unbelievably piddling. My reaction to most of the questions was 'So what?'. Meaningless items abound, such as 'How frequently is there a duplication of information in circulars and other 'for information/advice' paperwork sent by central government?'. Come again, Efficiency Scrutiny Unit?

There are belting ambiguities, like 'As far as your school is concerned, does paperwork arrive from central government at appropriate times?' with boxes to tick under the headings 'always', 'usually', 'rarely', 'never'. It all depends what they mean by 'appropriate'. Take this questionnaire masterpiece itself. It arrived in most schools in mid-March with a second class envelope. It had to be returned within about a week. This was 'appropriate', as they wanted the replies quickly, but so far as schools were concerned it was yet another chore.

Other questions are hilarious. 'Do you like our redesigned circulars?' Er yes, actually, changed my life they have. 'What have you done with the wall chart the DFE sent to all schools, entitled 'Education Act 1993 – Timetable of Publications'?' Do they *really* want to know? All right, we took down the Rembrandt and gave it pride of place in the hall.

I would love to see the replies to the section on information technology.

All the questions about laser printers and IBMs may not quite capture the reality of sellotape and ballpoints. So I have set up a rival outfit to the DFE Efficiency Scrutiny Unit. We at the Navel Scrutiny Unit will find out what really happens to paperwork with our own questionnaire.

1. When you see yet another wad of A4 papers in your morning post, do you:
a) say to yourself, 'Oh good. I really like paperwork'
b) go straight to the school office and give it to Doris so she can shred it
c) vomit

2. How much time do you spend each evening on paperwork?
a) under 3 hours
b) Over 3 hours
c) What is an evening?

3. What kind of information technology does your school possess?
a) New computers, with at least 300MB hard disc
b) An old coffee-stained BBC machine
c) A cracked Bic pen

4. What do you use for handling external paperwork?
a) The latest Microsoft Office software with E-mail
b) Doris's shoe box
c) We put it in the filing cabinet and pull the flush

5. What printers do you use?
a) 16-page-per-minute laser printers
b) An old Remington typewriter
c) John Bull Junior 2b printing set (with tweezers)

6. From which bodies do you receive paperwork?
a) SCAA
b) DFE
c) (North only) EYUPCHUCK
d) Age Concern

7. Do you like our new-look circulars?
a) Yes
b) No

Be fair, we spend a fortune on them, so write below what you think of us ...

8. Do Government communications render explicit the quintessential atomic elements of interactive mediation, and are the contextual features sufficiently transparent to facilitate expeditious comprehension?
a) Yes
b) You what?

9. (LEA schools only)
   Keep drowning us under even more bureaucratic bullshit. Please send us more more more. We love it
   Yes ❑

   (Grant maintained schools only)
   Just send us another million quid
   Yes ❑

10. Finally, draw a large circle on a big piece of sugar paper. Cut it out. Write the names of all members of staff on it. Then glue it to your bum.

Please mail your completed questionnaire to: The Navel Scrutiny Unit, Government Initiatives Plc, Futility Street, Unmitigated, Berks.

Times Educational Supplement 31.3.95

Free flannel with tender-soft soap

The first wave of bilge from the Teacher Training Agency has been washing around the newspapers. The TTA is the newest educational quango. It was set up, for no reason whatsoever, mainly to do what the Higher Education Funding Council already did, that is to dole out teacher training places, something it has not been handling especially well.

The TTA (motto: 'multus clueless') has been placing block adverts in the national press, under the heading 'Promotional Communication Services – Schoolteaching as a Profession – Invitation to Tender'. What on earth are 'Promotional Communication Services?', I hear you ask. Ah yes, of course. Promotional Communication Services are exactly the same as Fractilinear Flubbalubba Flangiforms. It's pretty obvious when you think about it.

Anyway, the Fractilinear Flubbalubba Flangiform division of the Teacher Trainspotting Aspidistra seeks the following, according to the adverts; 'The Teacher Training Agency invites tenders from suitably qualified companies or individuals to provide a comprehensive (oops, don't let ministers see that word!) programme of promotional and marketing services to promote teaching as a profession. The programme will involve the provision of literature and advice, advertising and regional support services'.

Aren't you sorely tempted to put in a tender? Would it not be glorious to be able counteract the usual public relations tosh that will be put out by commercial outfits? We at Flubbalubba PR, if our tender of £25 (including free flannel) is successful, will be offering a comprehensive, nay, a grammar school programme, of promotional and marketing services for the teaching profession that will tell it like it really is.

First, under that part of the tender requiring 'literature and advice', Flubbalubba PR will be offering ample amounts of both. Our 'literature' will consist of that premier collection 'Ministers' Greatest Hits'. This exciting pack will contain such mega hits as a re-issue, using the original

74

tracks, of 'The Government's Anthologee of Really Terrific English Literature for 14-year-olds', that topped the charts a year or two back.

Best piece of 'literature' of all will be that old 1991 favourite from the School Examinations and Assessment Council 'SEAC on the SATs', with its world class lyrics, such as 'For each attainment target, profile component and subject, check that the totals for D, N, W, 1, 2 and 3 add up to the total number of girls in year 2. For Ma 6 the totals for D, N, 1, 2 and 3 should add up to the total number of girls in Year 2. Repeat the process for boys'. Ah, they don't write lyrics like that any more. I'm still humming them.

Second, our 'advice' clinic is in the hands of a very experienced teacher, Mr Oldlagg. When potential recruits ring up, Mr Oldlagg will offer a snippet from his wide range of scintillating responses, like 'When you've been in teaching as long as me son...', 'Na, there's no call for that sort of thing nowadays', and 'Inner city schools? If you take my advice, love, you'll apply for a job as a swimming attendant in a pool full of piranha fish. It's safer'.

I am proud to unveil our national television advertising campaign. I'll admit that a little of its inspiration does derive from the current 'Papa' – 'Nicole' TV car ad, but it will, I am sure, be just what the TTA is not looking for. 'Nicole' is a primary teacher. You can tell that because the back shelf of her V-registered car is full of books she has taken home to mark. The rear seat is piled high with egg boxes she has scrounged from the local supermarket, so that her class can glue on six milk bottle tops, ten cornflakes and a piece of string and label them 'Star Ship Enterprise' (trendy technology project).

The back of her car is crushed flat from the many semi-literate motorists who have driven too close trying to read the rear window sticker that says 'If you can read this, thank a teacher – National Union of Teachers, Blackpool, 1981'. As the cheery car ad music tinkles away – dooby dooby doobedy doo, doobedy doo, doobedy doo – her engine coughs its way along, not through the French countryside, but down an inner city street, where it gives up the ghost and breaks down completely. While she explains to 'Papa' (the retired 'hit squad' head running the school since the Office for Standards in Education graded it 'unsatisfactory' and the real head had a nervous breakdown) why she is late for school, some spotty youths nick her hubcaps.

Our second TV advert does owe a smidgen to the National Lottery advertising campaign, which used various numbers in the landscape to persuade us that anybody could buy a ticket. First it shows a would-be teacher standing next to an aquarium. All the goldfish line up in a straight vertical line and a resonant voice says 'One. That's the percentage of your pay rise the Government will be willing to fund'. Next a dog barks. The would-be teacher turns to it and says 'Is that 'seven' or 'eleven'?', to which the dog replies, 'Either, mate. If you teach in a secondary school, that's the number of teachers likely to be made redundant. So after a year or two, it's 'woof woof' to you pal'.

The would-be teacher emerges from a tobacconist's shop clutching a bag of Maltesers (or 'the less fattening centres', as schools are called nowadays), and then he leaps high in the air. A giant hand appears out of the sky, points in the distance to a gloomy 19th century building with bars on the windows, labelled 'The Kenneth Baker Rest Home for Distressed Teachers', while a deep voice intones, 'It could be you'. The giant hand then waves two fingers at him, and he skulks off to the Job Centre.

Somehow I don't think we'll win the contract.

Times Educational Supplement 12.5.95

Whingers sight Upside Down Land

Now let me get this straight. On August 17th it was announced that the A level results had gone *up* by one per cent on last year. According to the 'Upside Down Law' postulated by the ranting right-wing, this proves that educational standards are going *down*. The exam is getting easier if the numbers passing it go *up*. Am I right so far?

A week later, on August 24th, the GCSE results were *down* by one per cent in English and maths compared with last year. So that must surely prove, according to this same Upside Down Law, er... let me just make sure I've got this right, that educational standards are *up*, because the numbers 'passing' GCSE are *down*? Have I finally grasped the rules of this complex annual sporting event? No, wrong again. Standards are still going down.

Forgive those of us whose brains cannot immediately take in the searing logic of it all, but I can see what is happening.

Each August a load of bath chair right wingers, (or 'right whingers'), are wheeled out to do their speaking clock act. The message is always the same and the actual exam results for that particular year are irrelevant. Standards are going to the dogs.

This annual farce enrages teachers and ruins the pleasure of thousands of hard-working and successful pupils and their families.

These critics must possess a special dictionary in which the English language assumes enormous flexibility. In this unique but handy lexicon, the words 'up', 'down', 'higher', 'lower', 'more' and 'fewer' all mean exactly the same as 'a barrel of dung'. So now you know.

Do not be surprised if a big dipper is installed in every school playground in the country, so that teachers can try and make sense of it next year while looping the loop.

To be fair the Government did try to cope with the mayhem. In this television comedy world, if John Major and Gillian Shephard are Basil and Sybil Fawlty, then brand new junior minister Lord Henley must be Bertie Wooster.

Anyway, Bertie trundled in front of the cameras, albeit with a look of total bewilderment on his face, to say that the pupils had done well. Good for him. When in trouble bring on the toff.

Not for nothing is August known as the silly season. It is the month when the Government publishes anything it hopes nobody will notice. In keeping with this time-honoured tradition, the report which thoroughly damned one of the Government's pet schemes – initial teacher training courses that have no higher education input – came out one midnight in mid August.

Another silly season story was John Major's Bank Holiday statement about more bribes for grant-maintained schools. According to chaos theory, if a gnat's wing flutters in Peckham, it could trigger a tropical storm in Brazil. There must be a second part to chaos theory which states that if a gnat's brain flutters in Westminster, it could set off a storm in the whole education system.

Poor old Major. His right wing was flapping so much during the Summer, small wonder he flew round in circles. In order to appease the rotating eyeballs faction of his party he had to make yet another comeback, one more even than Frank Sinatra. This time it was a front page story in *The Times* which implied that schools might be compelled to opt out.

Compelled to opt out? Now hold on a minute, Basil. You must have swallowed the right whingers' dictionary. I think the word 'opt' normally means 'choose'. By contrast, the word 'compel' is usually understood to involve no choice. Up, down. High, low. Choice, no choice. In Upside Down Land these opposites mean whatever you want them to mean.

Then there was a very exciting up-down seesaw, this time from Michael Heseltine. He announced with enormous pride a triumph for Government efficiency. He would ride to the rescue of beleaguered teachers and cut back ruthlessly on the bureaucracy going into schools. There was to be a reduction of millions of sheets of A4 being sent out by – none other than the Government.

Up, down, round and round. Who needs to crawl through all the August holiday traffic to the seaside and waste money on roller coaster rides, when this kind of thrill is available free? It was quite breathtaking. You *set up* a huge mess. You scale it *down*. Then you claim credit for rescuing people from your own bog-ups. Brilliant. Yet another example of the arsonists calling the fire brigade and then wanting a medal for it.

At the end of the month the recruitment figures for teacher training courses showed a drop of 28%, (or 'a half', as Kenneth Clarke would have put it). I wrote to the DfEE a few months ago pointing out that we would soon face an almighty shortage of teachers.

More pupils were coming into schools, I said, and graduate jobs would lead to a fall in recruits, as well as a drop out of disaffected teachers in their 20s and 30s. The reply was that there was no problem. If 'up' and 'down' are interchangeable, then I suppose there isn't one.

But the most emotional moment for me in August occurred when I was sitting in the library reading a newspaper. Suddenly my eyes caught the sad news that not only Kenneth Baker, but also John Patten would be standing down as a Member of Parliament in the next election. Up, down. In, out. Deeply moved by this shattering information I could not prevent a tear rolling down (or was it up?) my cheek.

Fellow readers looked across at each other, shuffled, and then stared at the floor, embarrassed by this tear-stained public display of profound emotion.

So I dabbed away the tears, stopped laughing, and carried on reading the rest of the paper.

Times Educational Supplement 8.9.95

Hotlines costing a donkey or two

Money seems to come in units of a quarter of a million pound nowadays, unless you are a hard-up school, that is. According to the annual accounts of the Department for Education and Employment, John Patten (who?) had 3,500,000 copies printed of a leaflet about testing children in schools.

When he changed his policy, these had to be junked. The cost of his little change of mind was a cool £250,000.

Nowadays such blunders have to be presented in a positive light, so the Treasury agreed to write off this six figure sum as a 'constructive loss'. The only true 'constructive loss' in recent memory was when Patten was given the elbow. If, in popular slang, £25 is a 'pony' and £500 is a 'monkey', then £250,000 will henceforth have to be known as a 'donkey'.

The Teacher Training Agency (a totally unneeded quango set up by, er, the same minister) has now hired a public relations firm to promote the image of the teaching profession at a cost of three 'donkeys'. Yes indeed. For a mere three quarters of a million quid of public money, people will be able to ring a 'hotline' and ask about the image of the teaching profession. 'Hot' will be the operative word. Can't you just hear the conversations?

'Hello. Is that the 'Teaching-is-a-breeze' Hotline? Can you tell me a bit about the wages and whether there's much stress in the teaching profession nowadays? Hello. Hello. Are you still there? Can you speak up, only there's a sort of spluttering sound on the line. Hello'. Brrrrrrrrrrrrrrrrrrrrrrrr........

I'm really glad that we have citizens' charters and these really helpful hotlines nowadays. Best not ring them on your mobile while you're driving along, however, as you might crash into a 'Cones Hotline' sign.

Perhaps, as a 'constructive loss', the two hotlines could be combined. 'Hello. Er, is that the Cones and Education Hotline? It's Gillian Shephard here. Look, I've got this double line of redundant ex-ministers outside my office. Can you send someone round to remove them? Only they don't seem to be serving any purpose. They've just been standing there for weeks and they're blocking the corridor'.

Another expensive wheeze is John Redwood's plan to spend £20,000,000 of public money, eighty 'donkeys' in new money, allowing popular schools to expand. I have never been sure how this Utopian idea would work out in practice.

It is all very well when an area needs additional school places, but what happens in regions that, if anything, have an over-provision? The same Government that is putting up the eighty 'donkeys' for expansion has been urging local authorities to take surplus school places out of use.

It will also be interesting to see what happens if schools that are popular because of their friendly intimacy, grow in size and become so big and impersonal that parents no longer want to send their children to them. Would the school then have to pay its share of the eighty 'donkeys' back again?

Perhaps the best idea would be for these expanding schools to build elastic extensions out of rubber. The new buildings could then be detached if the school ever became unpopular and bounce down the road to another palace of learning. Boing boing boing. Look out! Here comes a popular school. Boing boing boing. Oops! Oh dear, it's landed on the OFSTED inspection team.

Another expenditure of money that I found alarming was the introduction of £1,200 cash offers by a college attempting to persuade successful GCSE candidates to enrol in its A-level classes. Pretending this was just the same as university scholarships will not wash, as students actually apply for university awards, whereas these cash inducements were being offered to pupils who said they had already accepted places elsewhere. This kind of thing could cost a 'donkey' or two over the years.

If there is going to be a transfer fee scheme when pupils move up a stage, then maybe we should go the whole hog. Having a single rate is not good enough. What we need is competitive individual pricing, to reflect the true state of the transfer market.

Mavis Scattergood £1,500. Nigel Farnes-Barnes £800 (£1,000 if he wipes that smug grin off his face). Elsie Scroggins, £1 plus five national lottery scratchcards. Darren Rowbottom, minus £1,200 (his school pays another school £1,200 to cart him away).

The biggest source of cash bounties, however, will come later this academic year, when the pre-election giveaway is expected. A few weeks ago a front-page story in a national newspaper announced that there would be a billion pounds extra for education next year, or 4,000 'donkeys'.

Before celebrating, ask to see the true pedigree of this supposed bonanza. For example, millions and millions of pounds have been pulled out of the education budget this year, hence the many redundancies amongst teachers and the rapid growth in class sizes.

The Government did not meet the teachers' pay award. Universities are currently losing about ten per cent of their income. The air is thick with the deafening sound of donkeys' hooves, as whole herds are rounded up and corralled ready for the imaginary giveaway.

Add to this the cost of inflation. Four per cent of education's £20,000,000,000-plus national budget is near enough a billion pounds anyway. So it looks as if, one way or another, a couple of billion pounds has disappeared from the education spend already.

Now for the smart bit. You have had 8,000 donkeys taken away from you. Next year you will get 4,000 of them back. You will then be told you are 4,000 better off, when you are in fact 4,000 worse off.

Cheer up. After all, with donkeys in charge, it's only a 'constructive loss'.

Times Educational Supplement 22.9.95

Company cheapies teach teenies

From time to time an absolute belter of an idea scorches over the horizon and you just have to stand back and watch in breathless admiration.

Some of the best of these have emanated from that pointless quango the Teacher Training Agency, home of the teaching-is-a-breeze hotline and the very expensive PR campaign to improve the image of teaching.

Even better than these two winning ideas was a proposal from the Teacher Tragicomedy Agency at the end of the Summer, neatly headlined in the Times Educational Supplement as 'Company cast-offs to be lured into teaching'. Companies would be encouraged, said a TTA spokesman, to offer redundant employees a course of teacher training as part of their redundancy package.

Now hold on a minute, sunshine. Let us hear repeated loud and clear, and at regular intervals, that little phrase 'provided they are up to it'. There are some absolutely first-rate teachers who have been recruited from industry, amongst the best in the profession.

However, they were right for the job and usually took the initiative themselves, because they were motivated. There must be no blanket offers to all and sundry.

Perhaps at this very moment the prospect of being sent on a teacher training course is being used as a disciplinary tool.

'Ah come in Jenkins. I'm afraid we've not been very happy with your performance lately'.

'I'm sorry Mr Ramsbottom, only it wasn't my fault we had to scrap all those spigots'.

'Well it won't do Jenkins. As you know, we're about to be taken over by the Acme Spigot Company, so I was thinking.....'

'No, not the teacher training course, please Mr Ramsbottom. I promise to improve, honestly. I'll sweep the yard. I'll clean the toilets. But not the teacher training course'.

'It's too late Jenkins. You start at Swinesville College of Higher Education next Monday. Here's your first stick of chalk'.

'No, please Mr Ramsbottom, just one more chance. Aaaaaaaargh'. Jenkins hurls himself head first out of tenth floor window, as Mr Ramsbottom tries to hand him a stick of chalk embossed in gold with the words 'TTA Redundancy Scheme'.

Think of the interdisciplinary themes poor old Jenkins could have brought to the national curriculum. 'Spigots across the curriculum' – 'The history of the spigot' (history), 'Pitfalls in spigot manufacture' (technology), 'How many spigots make a dozen?' (maths), 'Spigot symbolism in the plays of Shakespeare' (English), 'L'importance internationale du spigot anglais' (modern languages). What a loss to the profession.

If shunting redundant industrialists into teaching is such a smart move, then why not operate the scheme in the opposite direction? Clapped out teachers could be offered a package to go into industry. Brilliant. This dredging of the dregs could be done by one of the TTA's twin bodies, the Teacher Draining Agency.

'Next please. Name?'

'Mrs Bea Wildered'.

'Problem?'

'I get terribly confused about marking the register'.

'Right. You're responsible for compiling the new privatised railway timetables. Next please. Name?'.

'Mr I. M. Knackered'.

'Problem?'.

'Er, I'm hopelessly out of date, I haven't a clue about modern education and I haven't read a book for years'.

'Good, good. Here's a list of educational quangos the Government will want to put you on. Next. Name?'.

'Ivor Goodlife'.

'Problem?'.

'Well, the head says I just want money for old rope, and whenever I open my mouth I keep putting my foot in it'.

'Excellent. Just what we're looking for. Water Board chairman'.

There is another imaginative possibility. According to George Walden MP, writing in the Evening Standard, the Government is currently deciding whether to put in its election manifesto a proposal to lower the school leaving age. Apparently the right-wingers want to turn the clock back 50 years by kicking 14 year olds out of school and sending them off into the workplace.

This offers the possibility of a really neat solution to the impending teacher shortage. Useless employees come out of the factories to enter schools as teachers, and Key Stage 4 pupils are sent into them at the age of 14, a bit like blood transfusions. It could become another stunning Government policy. Fire the creeps, hire the cheaps.

'Right, Year 10, pay attention please. My name is Mr Ramsbottom, and I'm the Managing Director of the Acme Consolidated (1995) Spigot Company. Now today you're going to .... Year 10, come on, pay attention, for goodness' sake. As I said, today you're all going to be making a lot of spigots'.

'Do we have to?'........

'Sir, Darren Headbanger's nicked my spigot'........

'Why us?'........

'I'm not doing it if there's any coursework' ....

'Please sir, I've got a sick note, sir'........

Good old right-wingers. Just what Britain needs to conquer international markets in the high tech world of the 21st century. It sounds like another cracking educational wheeze for the Teacher Straining Agency.

Times Educational Supplement 6.10.95

Five-fifths of mad cows read bullshit

I knew it. The public thought that the school curriculum and national testing had been simplified and teachers' lives had been made easy, but I always suspected that SEAC, the School Examinations and Assessment Council set up by the late great Kenneth Baker, had never been dismantled and was probably thundering away deep in some secret cellar, endlessly churning out incomprehensible test papers for seven year olds.

A report in the *Guardian*, headlined 'Ministry's emergency advisers', confirmed this dark suspicion, stating: 'The Spongiform Encephalopathy Advisory Committee (SEAC) meets twice a year but also convenes during emergencies. It is due to meet again in January to discuss the mad cow disease situation... The SEAC group, which is made up of senior brain experts, microbiologists and veterinary surgeons is due to be bolstered in the new year'. The report goes on to state that there is no reason for the public to panic.

Actually there is every reason for the public to panic. You see 'mad cow disease' is a *Guardian* misprint. It should have read 'mad curriculum disease'. Scientific research has now confirmed conclusively that this debilitating brain disease can be transmitted from politicians to human beings. When teachers were exposed to high levels of radiation from Government sponsored printed bullshit, many of them started lurching unsteadily, speaking in a slurred voice and cackling inanely at the sound of words like 'OFSTED'.

One problem for the teaching profession is that there is at least one report each week, and sometimes even one per day, on education. In less hysterical times this would be a good thing, but I am not aware of the same degree of insatiable scrutiny of other jobs. 'One third of dustbin emptiers drop rubbish on your drive', 'Forty-nine per cent of all chiropodists below average', 'Inspectors denounce mortuary attendants' are among numerous headlines I cannot recall ever reading in the national press.

Another problem is that the right-wing pressure groups in particular are very good at attracting publicity for their critical pamphlets, however flimsy, by issuing 'come-on' press releases. The newest right-wing think tank '*Politeia*' headlined its press release on Chris Woodhead's pamphlet criticising schools in block capitals with 'CHIEF INSPECTOR IN OUTSPOKEN ATTACK ON EDUCATIONAL THEORISTS WHO OPPOSE SCHOOLS REFORM'. Pretty low key, eh. I am thinking of starting my own right-wing think tank. To ensure media attention I shall find a catchy name for it, like Bollocks.

The biggest failure of our earlier educational system for older generations was that nobody seems to have taught anyone the meaning of words like 'norm' or 'average'. Most assessment systems of either teachers or pupils in use today are based on the idea of a normal bell-shaped distribution with lots of people in the middle and fewer at the extremes. When seven year olds were assessed for the first time, about a half scored at Level 2, while a quarter got Level 1 or Level 3. This gave rise to numerous headlines screaming 'A quarter of children below average' or '25 per cent fail test'.

When the Office for Standards in Education publishes figures about the assessment of teachers, the same applies to grades 4 and 5 on their five-point scale. The assumption by press and public is that nobody should be on grade 4 or 5. I agree entirely. All teachers should be highly competent. But can you imagine what would happen if this desirable state were to be reached? Let us suppose that 80% of teachers were given grade 1, 20% were awarded grade 2, while 0% obtained a 3, 4 or 5. There would be a huge outcry and a demand that all points on the scale should be used properly. The same would happen if all seven year olds scored at above Level 1 in national tests. The scale would have to be recalibrated so that those at the bottom obtained the new Level 1.

The result of these innumerable norm-referenced assessments is that debate about quality is often anaesthetised, as teachers reel under one critical report after another. The eventual reaction to this situation can be seen in some school districts in the United States, where over 80% of teachers are now graded 'truly outstanding', a category originally intended for the best 20% of the profession. Only the terminally naïve believe that almost all the teaching really is 'truly outstanding'.

A set of solutions for teachers who feel unfairly bludgeoned can be found, interestingly enough, in the official Government information pack sent to all schools about bullying amongst children. If applied to teachers instead of pupils, the information reads like a teacher union publication.

Under the heading 'When you are being bullied', it states: 'Be firm and clear – look them in the eye and tell them to stop... Get away from the situation as quickly as possible'. Good but unnecessary advice, Government. About three quarters of teachers are doing just that and retiring early.

The next section is entitled 'After you have been bullied' and the official advice is 'Tell a teacher or another adult in your school... If you are scared to tell a teacher or an adult on your own, ask a friend to go with you... Keep on speaking until someone listens... Don't blame yourself for what has happened'. Excellent advice for teachers, not just pupils.

I can just see the deputy head and sympathetic friend talking incessantly, while of course not blaming themselves, hoping Gillian Shephard will eventually appear and say, 'There there, it's not your fault'.

The title of this Government anti-bullying pack, by the way, is '*Don't Suffer in Silence*'. It deserves to take its place alongside the great classics on education, like John Major's book describing his vision of the future '*Tens and Units for the 21st Century*' and Chris Woodhead's pamphlet describing his vision of the future, entitled '*I Agree With You Entirely, Sir*'.

Times Educational Supplement 12.1.96

The token point of parental choice

'Ah, come in, sit down, do make yourself comfortable. My name is Arthur Tittle and I'm chairman of governors. It's Mrs Watson, isn't it?'

'No, I'm Mrs Wilkins. Mrs Watson was the lady before me.'

'Ah yes. I'm sorry about the mix-up, but we're interviewing so many prospective parents, it's terribly confusing. Still, we're down to our last vacant place. As you know, Mrs Wilkins, since the Government introduced more selection for secondary schools we now have to interview parents to see if they meet the high standards we the governors have set ourselves here at King Ethelred's Élite Academy, and ...'

'I'm sorry, Mr Tittle, I must be in the wrong place. I thought this was Gasworks Comprehensive. That's why I've come for interview, you know, about our Shane, to see if he can come here next September. Only he goes to Scumbag Primary at the moment, and I'd like him to come to Gasworks because it's our local school.'

'No, you're quite right, Mrs Wilkins, this used to be Gasworks Comprehensive until yesterday. But when the Government introduced more selection, we decided to change the school's name to something more 'up market' at our governors' meeting, to help us get the best recruits. The school is now known as King Ethelred's Élite Academy and we've set a fairly stiff selection test for parents'.

'Well, I didn't do that well at school myself, Mr Tittle, so I ...'

'Don't worry, Mrs Wilkins. I'm sure you'll do your best. Now the first question is, what do you and your husband do for a living?'

'I haven't got a job at the moment, but Mr Wilkins is a spoon finisher at Arkwright's. In fact, he's on late shift tonight, that's why he hasn't come with me.'

'A spoon finisher. Let me see. Forgive me a moment, I'm just looking it up on our chart to see how many points that gives you.'

'Points? I don't understand.'

'It's quite simple, Mrs Wilkins, we give parents a number of points for each item on our selection criteria. Being unemployed gets you no points, 'nul points' as they say in the Eurovision song contest, but your husband gets one point for being in a semi-skilled manual job. Now our next selection criterion is 'verbal reasoning'. Tell me, Mrs Wilkins, 'cat' is to 'kitten' as 'dog' is to ... what?'

'I don't understand, Mr Tittle, we haven't got a cat, and the dog's a bit deaf. But what's this got to do with our Shane coming to Gasworks, I mean King Ethelred's?'

'Look, let me repeat the question, Mrs Wilkins, it's a verbal reasoning intelligence test we're setting prospective parents. 'Cat' is to 'kitten' as 'dog' is to ... what?'

'Is it 'Spike'? That's what our dog's called'.

'I'm sorry, it's 'nul points' again, I'm afraid. The correct answer was 'puppy'. Now the last question is worth up to 100 points, so listen carefully. If your Shane came to King Ethelred's, how much would you be willing to contribute to school funds each year?'

'Oh dear, that's a bit hard to say. You see, his dad's been on short time at Arkwright's, but I spend £1 a week on a lottery scratch card, so if that came up...'

'Fine, Mrs Wilkins. Don't worry about it. Give us a ring if you win the big one. Thank you for coming for interview, and we'll be in touch.'.

'Oh, is that it, then? Only I hope you'll take our Shane. He's a nice lad, and I don't know where he'll go if he can't get in here.'

'We'll do what we can, Mrs Wilkins. You're the last person we're seeing, so please close the door as you leave. Right, ladies and gentlemen. That completes all the interviews, so let's just score Mrs Wilkins on each of our three criteria, and then we can make the final selection. I made it one point for social standing. All agreed? Good. Now what category do we put her in for the 'genetic endowment' criterion?'

'Can you just remind us of the categories, Mr Chairman?'

'I can indeed, Mrs Farnes-Barnes. The five categories are 'bloody clever', which scores ten points, then we go through 'clever' which gets five points, 'only think they're smart' which scores three, 'thick' gets one point, and 'monumentally stupid' gets zero. Shall we be generous and give her one point? Good, that's agreed. And clearly no points on our third criterion, 'filthy rich and suggestible', unless her scratchcard comes up. So a grand total of only two points for Mrs Wilkins, I'm afraid. Yes, Mrs Farnes-Barnes?'

'Can we just go back to the previous parents, Mr and Mrs Watson, because we gave them some bonus points which I didn't note down'.

'Yes, of course. Mr Watson came in a business suit, so that got ten bonus points. Then we awarded Mrs Watson fifteen extra points for her rather fetching black twinset and pearls, plus ten for wearing Miss Dior perfume. They got fifty points for coming in a Volvo estate, though we docked them five as it didn't have air conditioning. Then there was Mr Watson's additional ten for being captain of the golf club, and Mrs Watson's fifty points for her very fine elocution.'

'So the Watsons get our last place.'

'Correct, Mrs Farnes-Barnes. However, we still have one more duty. You remember that we decided it was important to be able to say to the press and public that King Ethelred's took pupils from all social backgrounds and abilities. Well we did hold back one place for this very purpose. I propose that Shane Wilkins is exactly what we are looking for, the perfect 'token prole'. I am sure, fellow governors, that the Government will be delighted with our brilliant implementation of their parental choice policy.'

Times Educational Supplement 26.1.96

A taste of terrible things to come

It is desperation time again. Despite the fact that some schools are currently laying off teachers, we are heading for the most enormous teacher shortages in the next few years. Look at the evidence. More and more children are coming into school each year, about 800,000 newcomers, compared with 650,000 to 700,000 in the age groups that are just leaving schools. Three-quarters of the current teaching force are quitting early, including 6,000 a year because of ill health, a figure that has trebled since the 1980s.

Applications to teach shortage subjects like maths and science are down by a quarter to a third compared with last year. When the economy picks up there will be even fewer applicants for training, and many disaffected teachers in their 20s and 30s will seek jobs elsewhere. So the Teacher Training Agency, a quango that is rather better at handling in-service training and recruitment than it is at dealing with initial teacher training (where the word 'useless' would be a kindness), is about to fling £1,600,000 at the problem.

A central feature of the proposed programme is a series of one-week 'taster courses' for people who might be interested in becoming teachers. Taster courses are a good idea. They may not be perfect, but they can give prospective applicants a few more clues than are found in glossy brochures about what the job entails.

Whenever I see the phrase 'taster course', however, I keep thinking of my driving test. As 18 year olds do, two friends of mine dreamed up what they thought was a hysterical wheeze, threatening to follow me round on my test run, fouling things up – braking sharply in front of me, shooting out of side roads, sounding their horn in annoyance, blocking the road when I tried a three-point turn. In the end they never did it, but I trembled all the way through, in case they did.

I keep seeing in my mind some hapless potential applicant on a taster course where the staff in the school do the same thing. As soon as the poor beggar arrives in a classroom one of the pupils is sick, right on cue. Another teacher, posing as the caretaker, enters, clutching a document purporting to be the agreement with the privatised school cleaning company, arguing that clearing up sick is not included.

At break time the deputy head, wearing a voluminous pair of incontinence pants, rushes into the staffroom clutching a letter, pretending the school has just heard of an impending inspection from the Office for Standards in Education, whereupon the head fakes a nervous breakdown (or has a real one, depending on the acting skills of the deputy). Then the village idiot, who is probably signed up as a lay inspector anyway, comes in posing as Chris Woodhead to tell the staff they will get grade 7, as they are all incompetent. A specially arranged school lunch of boiled cabbage and semolina follows. The taster week terminates after the first half day as the applicant flees down the drive to look for a more secure job with a bomb disposal unit.

There are certain aspects of teaching which are easily tasteable, like the boiled cabbage, and others with cannot be so instantly sampled. Teaching is for stayers, not sprinters, so the day-to-day reality of the job cannot always be demonstrated to order. Who knows when a pupil will ask a mind-blowing question, or whether an angry parent will burst into the school. More to the point, will the 'taster' manage to get a flavour of the whole job, including preparation, planning, marking, meetings, the odd quarrel, the shared laughs, the 'characters' on the staff, the talks after class with children, the routine and the exciting?

Perhaps the way to inform newcomers about some of these less readily visible aspects is to develop the sort of pretentious language of tasting that wine and food buffs use, to persuade them that only the most cultivated can appreciate the finer points of the job.

Marking books A deep and satisfying activity which can sometimes occupy many happy hours, at the end of which the suffusion of crenellated fingertips and leaking biro is indescribably sensuous and tactile.

Photocopying Modern reprographics are no match for time-honoured traditional methods, which allow teachers to savour the luxurious aroma of Banda fluid and Roneo stencils, transporting many away from the humdrum reality of classroom life into a carefree, consciousness-altering, transcendental world.

Official reports Pungently permeated with profound oriental mysteries, sometimes fruity, sometimes nutty, these rapturous treatises delight the intellect, with their rich vocabulary. Savour this veritable cornucopia of ineffable phraseology – 'Performance Criteria, Range Statements and Underpinning Knowledge/Understanding', 'End of Key Stage Descriptions', 'Flangified Splindongerous Breeblebats' – to name but a few.

Once the language of tasting has been established, then the obvious next step is to have an equivalent of the good food guides to help potential applicants find the right establishment to do their actual sampling.

Lower Swineshire College The peeling splendour of this school and community college has to be sampled at first hand to be fully appreciated. So many of our tasters have described this as 'typical', that it has been given the top Teacher Training Agency award of three spittoons for ambience. The head of science has won the Swineshire Staff Cynic of the Year award twice and will be scoffing for Britain in the forthcoming Eurovision Sneering Contest. Finish off your week's taster course with Friday afternoon's 'Duties of the Week' session, when the deputy head gives a live demonstration of how to dump all next week's unwanted duties on the newly qualified teachers.

On the other hand, with £1,600,000 to spend the Teacher Training Agency could give every teacher in the land a free tickling stick. The sight of smiling teachers would do more to recruit the next generation than a hundred other gimmicks.

Times Educational Supplement 3.5.96

Pass me another piano leg, Douglas

I have managed to get hold of the most sensational scoop. The only copy in existence of the new national curriculum for teacher training has come into my possession. It was found in an attic beside the long lost manuscript of a Mozart song. Both will shortly be sold at Sotheby's, and foreign buyers are expected from all over the world.

I am thinking of selling my unique copy of the national curriculum for teacher training to the British Museum for several million pounds, and having the Mozart manuscript perforated at six inch intervals, adding the slogan 'Now wash your hands'. Or was it the other way round?

The pedigree of the new national curriculum for teacher training is described on the back of the document. It was lovingly prepared by the Office for Standards in Education and the Teacher Training Agency, which is a bit like expecting two carrots to perform triple bypass surgery, but never mind, they have tried. The final version will eventually be validated by the Monty Python Appreciation Society.

The purpose of this Government curriculum for teachers is to restore finally and irrevocably to education the last missing jigsaw puzzle piece of the mythical Golden Age. In the 19th century teacher training institutions were called 'normal schools', because there was one single approved way to teach – the 'norm'. All teachers were fitted into the same straitjacket. In 1854, in his novel 'Hard Times', Charles Dickens wrote of Mr M'Choakumchild: 'He and some one hundred and forty schoolmasters had been lately turned at the same time in the same factory, on the same principles, like so many pianoforte legs'. It was a withering description of these 19th century clones.

By 1888 the Cross Commission was equally devastating in its condemnation of young trainees who had had a fixed repertoire of approved methods hammered into them: 'All they could do was faithfully to transmit the letter of the lesson they had received, for how should they have seized its spirit? Consequently all they were called

95

upon to do was to apply exactly the mechanical processes in which they had been drilled'.

Final examination papers reinforced the dreary sameness of it all. 'To what subjects would you apply Collective Instruction? What are the disadvantages of this method?'. A 1997 teacher training exam question suggested by Chris Woodhead? No, it is much too liberal for that, since it actually permits a discussion of disadvantages. It is in fact an exam question set for teacher trainees at St Luke's College in 1857.

Anyway, to return to this unique copy of the new national curriculum for teachers that has fallen into my hands, I can reveal that it has already caused a Government split. The Euro-sceptics want it to be called *Back to the Future*, while the Mad Cow Faction prefers *Forward to the Past*, but this is a minor matter.

The major purpose of this curriculum is to ensure that the 'normal master' idea of the nineteenth century is restored. Consequently all teachers will have to teach using the same methods, no matter what age group, subject or activity they are teaching. The essential ingredients are these:

Training institutions The Government will hand over both initial and in-service training to groups of estate agents, accountants and OFSTED lay inspectors. Other people with absolutely no knowledge of education may also be invited to bid for contracts.

Teaching methods The only method permitted is whole class teaching, irrespective of context. PE teachers will be shown how to teach fifteen a side tennis (five rows of three pupils either side of the net is the mandatory formation). Driving instructors will be taught how to give mass lectures on 'the clutch' or 'torque', instead of individual tuition.

Information Technology Computers and new interactive technology are supposed to individualise learning, but since this is outlawed, thirty pupils will have to sit in front of a single keyboard and screen, taking it in turns to use the mouse (Government-required method is for each pupil to have the mouse on the same day each month, so if your name is 'Montmorency', you probably get it on or about the 15th).

Teachers All teachers must be the same. In future every teacher, male or female, will be called Douglas. Any clothing worn must be in the official Government colour, grey. Teachers will be trained to start the school day by leading pupils in the singing of the new national anthem ('Woodhead save our gracious Queen, Woodhead save our noble

Queen, Woodhead save the Queen', etc). Teacher unions will be abolished and everyone will have to join the National Association of Pianoforte Legs.

Group work There won't be any. Drama lessons will consist of the chariot scene from 'Ben Hur' with the whole class either acting as members of the crowd or sitting in the chariot. Science experiments will be done in groups of thirty. Constructing the 'string telephone' will involve making a spaghetti-like telephone exchange with thirty pieces of string knotted together and everyone shouting at each other down them.

Projects Illegal, too trendy.

Qualifications All degrees and certificates for teachers will be abolished. Those successfully completing a course will have CLONE stamped on their forehead and be allowed to call themselves Douglas. Teachers embarrassed at the stigma will be permitted to cover their brow with a headband which has 'Vote Conservative' on it.

Actually I have made all this up. They don't clone people, they only clone sheep. And the Government wouldn't want that, now would they?

Times Educational Supplement 12.7.96

Santa sits down with the governors

It was a cold day in Snowland. Santa Claus looked out of the window wistfully as large snowflakes swirled round the playground of Snowland Primary School. It was the time of year when he wished he had never agreed to be chairman of governors. The December meeting was always scheduled for Christmas Eve, just when he had so much on his mind.

He had promised Mrs Claus he would be home by five o'clock, but the agenda was very full, so he knew he would not make it before seven o'clock. 'May we start please?', he began, as governors tried hard not to finish their sausage rolls, a Year 2 technology project that was more like a study in reinforced concrete.

The motley crew that made up the governing body of Snowland Primary School gratefully abandoned their half eaten, not quite up to Level 1 snackettes and slid into their chairs. There was the head, in the prime of his 'pre-retired' phase, eagerly angling for an early retirement deal, Mrs Plant, whose scalpel voice regularly shattered icebergs, Mr Oldfield, the bellicose staff governor, and one or two others.

'I think we'd better try to move quickly through the early items on the agenda', Santa began, 'as we've got quite a lot to get through'.

'I have several points to make under matters arising from the minutes of our last meeting', Mrs Plant intoned ominously. Santa sighed. A 'matter arising' from Mrs Plant could make the purchase of a bunch of daffodils for the school entrance seem like an issue of life and death.

'For example', she went on, 'Minute 103 (a) still does not make clear how much the school spent on books last year'.

'It was £10', Santa offered helpfully. 'Well £10 per pupil is simply not enough in this day and age', Mrs Plant replied, barely stoppable when in full flow. 'As a fully qualified OFSTED inspector, I.....'.

Santa switched off his hearing aid as Mrs Plant thundered on. She never let the governors forget that she had trained as a lay inspector.

It hadn't taken long. A few days in a hotel and she had got her badges for primary, secondary and special needs inspection. She had joined the Rentaprat inspection team on the personal recommendation of Henry

Rentaprat, the Chief executive and founder. She had been told she would only need the two day top-up course to be a fully qualified OFSTED brain surgeon and civil engineer as well.

'Not £10 per pupil', Mr Oldfield interjected angrily, '£10 for the lot. That's it. One single tenner. We spent it on a 'No talking' sign for the library. We might as well have invested a few pence buying a copy of the *Sporting Life* and put the rest on Kemptown Boy in the 2-30 at Chepstow. At least that would have trebled it'.

Santa's mind began to wander. Millions of presents had to be delivered within one night. He would never make it. He only had four reindeer and Wally and Plonker, the two junior ministers who had agreed to help out.

Gillian Shephard was down for an abacus with 60 beads on it, to help her count the number of pupils in each of next year's classes. Santa had no idea how he was going to get the abacus on to his sledge because it was thirty feet high, but Gillian Shephard had assured him that size doesn't matter. For John Major there was a left wing to go with his right wing, so that he could stop flapping round in circles.

'Can we concentrate on the agenda? We'll be here all night'.

Mr Oldfield's gruff and angry voice brought Santa back from his private thoughts. 'I wonder, Mr Chairman', the head oiled, with a deft smartness that belied his casting as Dopey in the school pantomime, *Snow White and the Seven Dwarfs*, 'if we could perhaps push on to the matter of my early retirement. It comes up under 'salary budget savings', item 6 on the agenda. Now although I am desperately keen to carry on as head, with just a little enhancement, perhaps eight added years, I might be persuaded....'.

Santa groaned inwardly. The head had been mentally in Provence for the last three years. His transparent master plan was to dupe the governors into topping up his years of service and then sail off to the Mediterranean in a brand new cabin cruiser called *Lump Sum*. There was a certain irony, Santa felt, as the head droned on. The school had to make cuts that the Government euphemistically called 'efficiency gains'. There was no greater efficiency gain to be had than the head hanging up his boots, but that would simply mean paying him off and then hiring someone else with greater verve than a potted dahlia.

'Mr Chairman ...'.

The last few empty lemonade glasses shattered as Mrs Plant rejoined the fray, moving into constitutional overdrive. 'I think we need a formal motion here, and any amendments to the substantive motion should be.......'.

Santa's brain began to turn to a fine mulch. Mrs Plant wanted to pass so many motions he wondered if she was on prune juice and syrup of figs.

He closed his eyes. Every year he asked himself why he had agreed to become chairman. He had an easy job, delivering a few billion presents in a couple of hours, so why take on a hard one like being chairman of governors? Perhaps he should just resign and leave education to the politicians.

As the snow swirled round the windows of Snowland Primary School, he watched Wally and Plonker, the two junior ministers, pooling their massive intellects to try and decide whether the sledge pulled the reindeer, or the reindeer pulled the sledge.

Santa thought it over for a nanosecond and then decided to stay on as chairman after all.

Times Educational Supplement 15.12.95

Chapter 4
Life in the classroom

Pale imitators of the imagination game

Woody Allen once said that every time he got into a lift, it took him down to the basement and beat him up. The feeling that technology has a mind of its own, is beyond human control, and may well turn peevish and malevolent, is what prevents me from believing that teachers will one day be unnecessary.

That teachers might be dispensable is a beguiling thought to politicians. There is the faint hope that at least one of the new technologies will eventually sideline teachers. Think of the benefits to the Government if the teaching profession did not exist and children were taught by machines. Since salaries account for some eighty per cent of a school's annual budget, as much as ninety per cent in small schools, billions of pounds would be saved.

Machines do not belong to professional associations, so there would be no threat of industrial action by the National Union of Virtual Reality Kits. There is no chance of computers boycotting Key Stage 3 SATs, just because the British Federation of English Assessment Software Packages takes a dislike to the Government's Anthology of English Literature. I cannot see screen messages appearing, saying 'Government philistinism rejected. Access denied'.

'Ah, but can machines do the important things in education?', I hear you ask, 'like pick up litter, play cards in the staffroom, decide whether Darren Rowbottom hit Elspeth Scattergood first?'. Well they can pick up litter, and distinguishing crisp packets from A4 paper is no problem, but deciding between a paper that has been deliberately discarded and one that has fallen on the floor accidentally, might be. So it could be goodbye both to old versions of the national curriculum and this year's draft budget.

Playing cards and chess is not difficult, as there are plenty of good quality programs around, but what makes staffroom games worthwhile, like watching the losers burst into a torrent of profanities, might be more elusive. Sorting out tiffs between Darren and Elspeth would be beyond machines unless a human were present, as children would either switch them off, ignore them, or, nowadays, re-programme them. The biggest advantage of computerised schools would be that machines don't cry when OFSTED calls.

You can see how the possibility of never needing teachers again comes to be raised. Technology is a tease. Whenever a new form is developed, the manufacturer invariably over-hypes its possibilities. In the 1920s radio was first used in schools. The reaction to the first broadcasts was that schools would one day have a box in every classroom and teachers would be redundant. Television provoked the same response – who needs teachers when David Attenborough can tell children all they need to know about insects?

In the 1960s, when elementary teaching machines were developed, it was said that this really was the beginning of the end for the teaching profession. Behaviourist learning theory was supposed to have shown that children learn best in small steps, with self-pacing, active responding, immediate reinforcement and feedback. Unfortunately, nobody ever told the pupils that this was supposed to happen, so most threw up at the brain-corroding banality of endless piddling globs of information with silly, self-evident questions every few seconds.

In the 1980s the microcomputer was expected to do what 1960s teaching machines had failed to achieve, but, like other forms of technology, it simply took its place alongside teachers, rather than replaced them. Now, as the 21st century dawns, interactive technologies, like CD ROMs, Virtual Reality and the information superhighway, are supposed to be poised to deal the final death blow to the teaching profession.

According to the Government view of teaching, this should not be too difficult. After all, in their simple-minded perception of the profession, anyone in possession of the subject knowledge of the national curriculum can teach it, no training is necessary. Also, any fool can assess either teaching or learning, since ticking boxes is not exactly mind-stretching. Teaching is supposed to consist solely of imparting information, so the superhighway, the ultimate repository of the world's films, sound records, texts, only has to be switched on.

But information is not knowledge. It takes skill to get the stuff from out there into someone's head. Fortunately the attempted de-humanisation of teachers in recent years has not worked. Despite all the box ticking, most teachers have clung on to their craft skills. There is still some imagination in the profession, and though the critical faculties of some teachers may have been dulled, there are many who think for themselves and encourage children to do the same, and that is what frightens politicians.

I once watched a superb music lesson, as the teacher tried to encourage small children to interpret a particular song. 'Spread jam on it', she eventually said. It was just right and achieved the desired effect. I am not sure by what century machines will have that sort of distinctive individual and spot-on response. Then there was the maths teacher who was so enthusiastic he ran maths clubs, got families to tackle maths problems and made a subject which many find frightening, a source of inspiration. Machines hold the content, but none has the personal charisma, even when programmed in an off-beat and amusing way.

A few years ago Frank Muir and Denis Norden invented a character called Rudolph. He was a foreign spy whose job it was to sabotage British life. When nothing comes out of a tomato sauce bottle, you bash it underneath. It then explodes all over your plate. That was the work of Rudolph.

The ultimate reason why technology will never replace teachers is quite simple. A few years ago Rudolph moved into new interactive technology. Day after day he sits there just waiting to bog everything up. If you doubt that, then ask yourself this. If OFSTED descended tomorrow to watch a carefully planned lesson based on new interactive technology, wouldn't you put your mortgage on it breaking down?

Times Educational Supplement 14.4.95

Carpetbagging for beginners

The other day I received a strange letter. It thanked me for my application for a teaching post and then consoled me for not getting it. There was only one problem. I had never applied for the job, though I had acted as a referee for a former student who had. In a very confused office somewhere, a whole pile of applicants, referees, and, for all I know, suppliers of fine stationery, board dusters and plastic bin liners, were being sent the same computer-generated personalised blessing.

The last time this happened I wrote to the school concerned saying that, even though I had not applied for the post of girls' PE teacher, and had only written a reference for a candidate, I was now so mortified at the disappointment, my self-esteem would never recover. A few weeks later I received a letter addressed to 'Ted Wargg' apologising for the error and blaming a 'temp' for the momentary lapse in standards. You just can't get the staff nowadays.

It all seemed to illustrate the chaos that exists in many establishments, not just schools, as more professions become mobile rather than permanent. Armies of temps, clutching their copious holdalls, now inhabit broadcasting, publishing, teaching, the health service, and numerous other jobs that used to pride themselves on the devotion and calibre of their permanent staff. Some members of the Government like this crude manifestation of 'the market' and want every teacher to negotiate an individual annual contract, which would produce even more armies of carpet baggers roaming around looking for a post. Any teachers having business cards printed should insert the slogan 'Have chalk – will travel'.

Cuts in education funding, increasing sickness amongst teachers, individual annual contracts if they ever come about, will make teaching an increasingly footloose profession. More and more teachers, in pursuit of short contracts, will find themselves hawking their wares like tinkers around interviewing committees. This will spawn a new breed of itinerant professional – mobile, smart at answering interview questions, well scrubbed and polished. Some itinerants have achieved high office, slipping deftly in and out of jobs just before they were rumbled.

The problem with the shift to more short-term appointments is not just the difficulty of rumbling a charlatan at interview, it is what inevitably goes with the stop-gap approach to teaching or any other profession. First of all there is no clear career path. People can go up and down like a roller coaster, soaring up to a post of high responsibility one day, then being made redundant and having to take any old job to pay the rent the next. Secondly, much more pressure falls on the so-called permanent staff, as they have to solve the serious problems, deal with parents and the community, plan ahead.

Many people on the short contract circuit are of course excellent teachers, sometimes forced into mobility by circumstances, and woman teachers in particular, however brilliant, have often interrupted a successful career and found themselves having to trek round temporary jobs on their return. The down side of short-termism, however, is that solidly virtuous teachers do not necessarily shine in interview, and some successful new breed itinerants, though clever interviewees, are as hollow beneath the surface as an Easter egg and just as likely to melt when it gets hot.

Having sat in on a few interviews over the years I have seen some of the more stylish tinkers at work. The Smarmpot charms round the interviewing panel, often targeting the opposite sex. Experts manage to avoid plonkingly obvious crudities, such as 'may I congratulate you on your superb dress sense', which in any case does not go down too well with a chairman of governors clearly dressed in what looks like a potato sack. The Smarmpot often flatters by agreeing with the questioner, however banal the question – 'Do you like children?', 'That's a very important question...', rather than, 'Come off it, sunshine, is the Pope a Catholic?'.

The Assassin stalks the opposition, picking off the rest of the shortlist one by one. I remember one Assassin who had very expressive facial features. In the period before the formal interviews, when the candidates were being shown round and talked to informally, he never actually said in so many words that the ideas being put forward by the others were useless. He just kept raising his eyebrows quizzically and wrinkling his nose, as if their suggestions were outrageously impractical.

The Oracle remains silent and then gives short intriguing answers. This only works with the right sort of selection committee, but phrases like 'There are certain resonances...' or 'It depends where you're coming from...' do seem to go down well with some panels. Personally I have always assumed, wrongly perhaps, that if people have anything intelligent to say they will say it, rather than weave a web of Sanskrit around it. However, with some interviewing bodies empty gibberish may succeed, so, for the more gullible, it might be worth practising phrases like, 'The moon never lights a dark valley', or 'Give me a child until he is 46 and I will show you the man'.

The Fireball enthuses about every issue that comes up – been there, seen it, done that – sometimes claiming to have direct personal experience of so many initiatives you wonder if he ever did the same thing twice. One Fireball tried to impress the interviewing committee that she had read every book on every new idea in education and was clearly a much more reflective practitioner than any other applicant. The chairman then asked her to describe one book that had particularly influenced her practice, at which she looked dumbfounded and imploded.

Politicians sometimes justify short-termism, annual contracts, temporary appointments and the 'market' approach, by saying that this is how they themselves have to operate – election candidate one day, MP the next, Minister of Brain Surgery the day after. A fat lot of good that system has done us.

Times Educational Supplement 28.4.95

You don't have to be mad to try this ...

The announcement by Gillian Shephard of a proposed new qualification for head teachers has again raised questions about what society should expect from the holders of these crucially important posts. Some of my best friends are heads. 'Ah yes, but would you let your daughter marry one?', someone called out when I said this at a conference.

The demands on heads have escalated in the last few years. Many heads lament not being able to teach children as often as they used to, or having less time to discuss with staff what is happening in the classroom. As business-type demands have grown, so the time and energy available for other vital matters has eroded.

When teachers show interest in becoming a head, some kindly older hand usually takes them on one side and lets them talk until they get over it, like the Samaritans do. 'Thanks for listening to me, Brian. Only I was feeling depressed, so I wasn't sure whether to run under a bus and end it all immediately, or apply for a headship and take a bit longer'.

The feeling that you have to be daft nowadays even to contemplate becoming a head is not exactly new. Talented though most heads are, there has always been a streak of eccentricity in the pedagogical equivalent of the 'Barmy Army'. One girls' grammar school headmistress used to close the school down for three days so that everyone, staff and pupils, could make marmalade, which was then sold to raise school funds. It was a brilliant idea. Nowadays she would get a CBE.

An ex-Navy head believed that the school was his ship, so he baffled staff and pupils with references to 'aft' and 'cabins'. Another engaging nutter rode on his bike up and down the school corridors. Then there was the head who read out long harangues to the staff once a week, oblivious to the fact that most, and on some occasions all, had left the room as soon as he opened his mouth.

Everyone who has worked in more than one school has a tale or two of endearing eccentricity. It has almost been a prerequisite for the job. What concerns me about recent developments, however, is that we are not using as effectively as we should the considerable strengths which good heads can bring to their schools.

By drowning them under brain-corroding bureaucracy, the Government has sidetracked them. The BBC made the same mistake when it announced that radio and television producers would be encouraged to study for a higher degree. But it was not an MA in creative arts, film making or radio they were to take, but rather a Master of Business Administration. Dreary.

So I hope the Government does not make the same mistake with its new qualification for head teachers, the Dip. Head, or Dip. 'ead, as it will no doubt be known. The most important duty of heads should be to enhance the quality of teaching and learning in their school. One of the best heads I have ever met was principal of a New York high school with 7,000 pupils. He could have spent all his time on paperwork, or with the police, for the area had a horrendous crime record. Yet almost every day he watched and discussed a lesson with one of the school's 375 teachers. That, he said, was his top priority.

I suspect that the Dip. 'ead will be dominated by bureaucracy, so I have composed the exam paper for the first cohort. Don't laugh. The DFEE is already photocopying it.

Government Dip 'ead – Final Examination Paper
Time allowed – 3 hours, or a lifetime, whichever is shorter

1   Compare and contrast the stupendous achievements of the following educational giants: (a) Kenneth Baker (b) Kenneth Clarke (c) Basil Fawlty (d) Daffy Duck. Say which two should be sanctified.

2   Your school is housed in a clapped out leaky building and your science lab only has three magnets, two magnifying glasses and a one metre ruler in its stock room. Write a description, in fluent Estate Agent Speak, telling prospective parents what a wonderfully equipped palace the school is.

3   Choose one from the following list of classics: 'War and Peace' (Tolstoy), 'Pride and Prejudice' (Austen), 'Great Expectations' (Dickens), 'Choice and Diversity' (Patten). Compare the classic you

have selected with your school development plan, stating which is the greater work of fiction.

4   You are able to appoint two deputy heads. Describe which of the following major areas of senior management responsibility you would assign to each one: (a) curriculum (b) pastoral care (c) picking up litter (d) all the crappy jobs I don't want to do.

5   A local pork pie manufacturer offers your school a generous amount of cash sponsorship, provided you will promote his products. Either (a) map out an interdisciplinary project entitled 'Pork pies across the curriculum', or (b) design a pork pie shaped gymnasium.

6   You have to make several teachers redundant. Explain and justify the major principles on which you would base your decisions, choosing one of the following criteria: (a) incompetence (sack the least skilful teachers) (b) salary cost (get rid of the most expensive staff) (c) settle old scores (see off the buggers you can't stand any more).

7   (Practical test) Take the sow's ear provided in the plastic bag. Turn it into a silk purse (at zero cost).

8   ('Barmy Army' index) Please tick one of the following. I am:
(a) entirely sane, therefore ineligible for the award.
(b) slightly eccentric, but could become barmy should the need arise.
(c) a petunia. Dooby dooby doo. Send me my badge.

Times Educational Supplement 20.10.95

Rage against the vying of the bright

Have you had a 'rage' lately? Rages are all the rage nowadays. If you get cut up by a fellow motorist, so you decide to lob your car jack through his windscreen at the next traffic lights, then that is apparently all right. You are simply suffering from 'road rage'.

No problem either if, after standing in line at the supermarket checkout, you decide to tip your frosties over the head of the cashier, abandon your brimming trolley and storm out. Just a touch of 'queue rage'.

If you want to make something which is rather distasteful appear to be acceptable, then just give it a fashionable name. Psychopaths must love it. 'Sorry I went berserk with the machine gun, m'lud. Slight attack of 'people rage' I'm afraid'. 'No problem. You are merely a victim of *furor humanitas*. Case dismissed'.

Recently I have been wondering why more teachers are not suffering from 'career rage'. The steady professional ladder of promotions from fresh-faced rookie to head teacher is eroding. If it is increasingly respectable to argue that the blind mist of anger is an excuse for violence, then why are the court case columns of newspapers not full of teachers venting their ire for having their career opportunities blighted?

It can begin at the interview stage. There are several horror stories of the antics of chairmen of governors who have decided that they will personally de-brief unsuccessful candidates after an interview. Some chairmen are very good at this, sensitive and helpful, striking just the right note.

The dimwits, unfortunately, are clueless. 'Your referees let you down', one trilled, spilling the detail to an unsuccessful candidate. She immediately hot footed it to her hapless reference writers, who mistakenly believed that they had written in confidence.

Another chairman thought the direct approach was best. As the interviewing panel and applicants munched their refreshments afterwards, he took each unsuccessful applicant aside. 'We decided you weren't up to it', he announced to one, 'you just haven't got enough oomph'.

The chairman was then carried out to nearest accident and emergency unit for the surgical removal of a plate of sausage rolls, as the candidate suffered an attack of oomph, or 'prat rage' as medical science calls it. Except that he didn't. Like others in similar circumstances he just went home and complained to his friends at his treatment, in the best long-suffering tradition of the profession.

It is astonishing how impotent some teachers now feel about their career. Part-timers are laid off, supply teachers find their pay rates cut, full-timers are made redundant after years of service. Occasionally there is a protest march, but outside of a small circle of close friends and colleagues, few in the wider society seem to want to do anything about it.

One very significant step in the career ladder is being eroded as the number of deputy headships declines. Schools in the red often do not replace deputy heads who leave, to save money. Their work then falls on the shoulders of the head and other teachers. An important job, and a valuable training ground for many future heads, is under threat.

There is a sad game that has been played out at a number of colleges of further education. It is called 'pass the parcel'. One Saturday a motor bike courier calls at the teacher's door bearing a buff envelope. What exciting treat could this be? An unexpected windfall? An unclaimed lottery prize? An early Christmas present?

No, it is none of these. It is actually a redundancy notice. In some cases the teachers were told that they must clear their desk immediately, but only if escorted round the premises by a member of the security staff. Most victims go numb rather than wild.

I suspect that many teachers avoid career rage by using defence mechanisms like this. The well-known defence mechanisms, such as 'regression' and 'sublimation', were neatly laid out by Sigmund Freud. They are alive and well in the teaching profession.

'Regression' involves returning to one's childhood to regain a sense of security – 'Disappointed at missing promotion? Me? Don't make me laugh! Er, would you mind passing me that teddy bear and blanket please?'.

Other people practise 'sublimation'. This is the avoidance of rage by channelling aggression into something higher and nobler, thereby gaining respect from oneself and others – 'As I failed to get that senior post I shall simply dedicate all my energies in future to supporting a worthwhile national institution. Such as the brewing industry'.

Another favourite is 'displacement', which occurs when people divert their anger away from the thing they really hate towards something else instead, like a scapegoat – 'No, I wasn't upset when the chairman told me I lacked oomph. I blame Margaret Thatcher'.

We can learn a great deal about coping with rage from the natural world. Konrad Lorenz, who won the Nobel Prize for his studies of animal behaviour, wrote a marvellous book about dogs. He describes the ritual when two aggressive male dogs meet. If they are both on the leash they tend to strain and snarl at each other in an impressive display of rage, knowing that they do not actually have to fight.

When dogs are off the leash, however, they are much more pragmatic. They approach each other, slide by, sniff one another, and then, honour satisfied, urinate gracefully against the nearest tree and go home.

So there you have it. If you don't get that bonus, should you be pipped at the post for that headship, if the chairman of governors tells you that you lack oomph, then worry not. Don't throw a fit, don't stamp and rage, don't push your blood pressure up to danger levels. Just nip quietly outside and tiddle on the geraniums.

Times Educational Supplement 17.11.95

Vinnie Jones for chief inspector, OK?

Did you see that notorious advert for state schools which appeared in the press recently? It was published under the banner headline, 'Problems in private schools worry parents', and the text stated: 'The educational crisis surrounding the teaching standards in private schools has been heightened by recent press reports of drug and sex scandals in them. We all know that teachers in state schools have to be properly trained, while those in private schools do not, so the real casualties are the pupils'.

Rather below the belt for local authority schools to advertise themselves by rubbishing their private school counterparts, don't you think? What's that? You never actually saw this shameful newspaper advert? Well neither did I, because I just made it up. It is based on a real advert for private schools which used similar innuendo about state schools.

In the advertising trade this is known as 'knocking copy'. It is the 'Brand X' style of ad that either directly or obliquely attempts to undermine its competitors. The tag line reads something like: 'Wizzo cleans a lot better than some washing powders we could mention'. Nudge nudge.

A few years ago I complained about the private sector in education resorting to the same shabby tactics, by paying for whole page adverts, and in some cases several page supplements in local and national newspapers, and then knocking the state system in the accompanying piece of deathless prose which extolled the virtues of private education. The fact that there is a discreet flag at the top of the page saying 'Advertising feature' is neither here nor there, as the whole text is set out in exactly the same style as the rest of the newspaper, making it look as if it is part of its normal editorial content.

I was sad to see the resurrection of this sleazy way of drumming up customers for private schools in a local newspaper, where, under a banner headline reading 'Classroom conflicts make parents think again', the following opener appeared: 'The educational crisis surrounding the teaching standards of state schools have (sic) been heightened by recent press reports of falling standards in classrooms. While teachers and the government draw the battle lines over the National Curriculum and funding, the real casualties are the pupils who are suffering poorer educational standards'.

Nasty, eh? The imagery is rich with the language of war – 'battle lines', 'casualties', 'suffering'. The problem is that a hostile attack like this will provoke an aggressive response. If the advertisers of private schools have become so desperate that they revile teachers in maintained schools who are doing their best against the odds, then they must not grumble if the same happens in reverse one day – 'We all know what happens to teachers who get fired from state schools for fiddling the accounts – they get jobs in private schools', or 'Do you want your child to be normal, friendly, sociable, or do you want an unspeakable toffee-nosed prig? Well if it's the pretentious snob you're hoping to raise, then there's not much doubt where you should be sending him ....'.

What is particularly disappointing about this recourse to aggressive defamation is that there is no need for it. At both national and local level, good independent schools have lived harmoniously with their local authority counterparts. The heads of many independent schools have not been afraid, in their national conferences, to speak up on behalf of their state school colleagues. At local level there are numerous examples of friendly relationships. Someone should publicly disown the knocking approach to recruitment before it becomes established again.

The Government must love this aggressive dog-eat-dog free market stuff. It is exactly what the right-wing wants to see. The strong triumph by any means possible, the weak go to the wall. Except that it is not a free but a rigged market, with the Government interfering at every turn. The latest wheeze from John Major is to allow grant-maintained schools to borrow more money, using their buildings as collateral. Not that this actually gives them anything, other than a bigger debt. All of which goes to show that Major, living up to his reputation as a dolt over education, cannot even manage to fudge properly.

Perhaps the state sector should fight back. If competition and the market are so good at raising standards, then why can we not set up a privatised Government in competition with the present bunch of incompetents? I suppose this is a bit like asking why there is only one Monopolies Commission, but some stiff competition for the

Government would not come amiss. Norman Wisdom could be the privatised Prime Minister, so the quality of clowning in that office would improve, the speaking clock could become parallel Education Minister, thereby upping considerably the intellectual level of thinking in that department, and footballer Vinnie Jones would make a first-rate privatised Chief Inspector of schools, showing OFSTED how to tackle incompetent teachers without leaving a mark.

The state sector could run a national advertising campaign. Every evening, at peak viewing time, television commercials would extol the virtues of state schooling. Instead of the well-known milk chocolate ad, viewers would see Harry Ramsbottom, fearless teacher of Year 10 at Little Piddlington School and Community College, swinging across ravines, skiing along the edge of avalanches, climbing up steep walls. But he is not delivering a box of chocolates.

After all the private school advert hype about 'battle lines', 'casualties' and 'suffering'; after teaching forty pupils in a leaking classroom with less than £10 per head to spend on his pupils' books; after being comprehensively rubbished by *Panorama* and every other newspaper or broadcast feature in the land, he is just desperately trying to get through the snow drifts to attend a one day school-based INSET stress management course on 'Sex for the debilitated'.

Times Educational Supplement 1.12.95

Top of the pork-pie league tables again

Swinesville School
Parents' Newsletter No 66

Dear Parent,
It barely seems a month since I wrote my last parents' newsletter to you. It's certainly a busy life being Head of Swinesville School nowadays. Time absolutely flies. Yes, a whole month. That's 31 days.

Yes indeed. Another 744 hours have passed since I penned my last month's 'View from the Head'. That's 44,640 minutes of action-packed school life, with barely a second to draw breath, let alone calculate that it's actually 2,678,400 seconds since I sent Newsletter No. 65 to you. There's so much been happening I hardly know where to start.

Staff leavers

Mrs Spellbinder, Head of English, left us at the end of last term. The governors have frozen the post to help cover our deficit.

Mr Nackered, Mrs Dunfore, Miss Haddit and Mr Shaggedout have all retired early to the Kenneth Baker Rest Home (no visitors for six months, please, doctor's orders).

Mrs Jewell, Mr Supreme and Miss Starr (all special needs) have been made redundant.

New staff

We welcome the following new appointments: Mr Prisonwarden as truancy officer, to help us climb up the Swineshire Piggeries Truancy League; Mrs Vampire, formerly Bursar at Count Dracula Private Academy, to be in charge of fund raising.

To temporary posts: for one month – Miss Klinsmann (German); for one week – Mr Syd Lexia (Spelling); for one hour at a time, renewable – Mr Rambo (Year 11, non-GCSE).

Staff responsibilities

Following the recommendations made by school inspectors last term I have decided to reorganise some staff duties.

Teachers will in future have the following changed titles and responsibilities: Mrs Hangglider, formerly Deputy head, to be Vice Principal (Waste Paper Collection and Car Boot Sales); Mr Strangler (Deputy head) to be Vice Principal (Discipline and Excluding Troublemakers).

Miss Gravitas (Head of maths) will be Assistant Principal (League Tables, Legal Assemblies and the Parent's Charter).

Mr Airhead (Woodwork and gardening) will become Total Quality Assurance Officer.

Governors

Congratulations to Mr Gerrymander who was elected parent governor with 8,975 votes, and to Mrs Apathy who was elected staff governor with 2 votes (73 abstentions).

Mr Chump has again been elected Chairman of governors, and Mrs Chump is once more Vice-chairman. Parents and pupils of the school will thus still qualify for ten per cent off a pork pie at the Chump Meat Emporium.

All you have to do is produce a school cap or beret, and then sing the local commercial radio jingle 'Fly high high high with a Chump pork pie'.

There have been various co-options to the governing body this term who will be a help with the commercial and political side of education: Mrs Spigot (Acme Ballcocks) brings welcome industrial experience; Mr Palmgrease (Palmgrease Parliamentary Lobbyists) and Miss Spanky (Libido Theme Parks Plc) have good contacts with Swineshire MPs.

Curriculum and testing

Many parents have phoned about the Swinesville Echo report 'Dearing frees one day a week' to ask if we could make it Friday, so the family could get away for a long weekend. The Dearing Committee simply reduced the National Curriculum to 80% of the week, so no specific day is actually free.

Some parents have written asking why my last newsletter said that we were top of the examinations league, when the Swinesville Echo table showed us in 56th place out of 57 Swineshire schools.

It is important to remember that these are unadjusted raw league tables, very crude indicators indeed of true achievement. What is important nowadays is 'value added'. When we recalculated all the scores to remove the effects of the small size of our playground, the many teachers off with a bad cough, severe depletion of the ozone layer over Swinesville, age of central heating boiler, children in other schools having learned a lot more than ours, and then took away the number we first thought of, Swinesville School actually came top of the league.

Parent-Teacher Association Finance
I am pleased to report that, after a long meeting of the Finance sub-committee of the PTA, it was decided that the £100 raised by parents should be invested.

Using a combination of the chairman of governors' IQ, the proportion of GCSE high grades obtained last summer, and the percentages in the mock exams of our four A-level candidates, the numbers 8, 9, 16, 21, 24 and 27 will be backed in the National Lottery each week for the next two years.

School events this term
Illegal morning assemblies will be held in the Chump Meat Emporium Building on Mondays to Thursdays and legal assemblies on Fridays.

February 8th – Sex education video will be shown.

February 9th – For parents who have withdrawn their children from sex education classes there will be a talk entitled 'Keeping the Thingy away from the Whatsit'.

As ever I am grateful for all the support from parents of Swinesville School, though anything that can be done to improve the gene pool would be greatly appreciated.

I. ANDROID BA, TQA AND BAR
BS EN ISO 9001, CHIEF EXECUTIVE

Times Educational Supplement 20.1.95

Year of the Twerp and Big Chief I-Spy

After attempting to work out who won the educational accolades and booby prizes for the year just ended, I think it must have been the Chinese year of the twerp.

The top prize for the most breathtakingly silly public statement of 1995 must go to Gillian Shephard for insisting that class size does not matter. If there is one parent or teacher in the land who would swap a class of twenty for a class of forty, then I have yet to meet them.

Gillian's prize is to do a national curriculum technology project with a primary class of forty and no money for the necessary equipment and materials.

I have little time for the man, but I would offer a can of lager and a big cigar to Kenneth Clarke for having the courage to resist a too outrageous tax giveaway, despite the pressure from his own back benchers. The 800 million pound so-called 'windfall' in the autumn budget was only a fraction of what has been taken out of the kitty in the last couple of years, but schools could have been even worse off. Unfortunately further and higher education came off very badly and start 1996 marooned well up Excrement Creek.

The prize for persistence must go to former junior education minister, Big Mike Fallon. I shed a crocodile tear every time he got turned down for yet another constituency, but he kept popping back up off the floor like those inflatable punchbags that you smack hell out of.

I would love to don a false beard and dark glasses and pose as a potential candidate at one of these selection meetings. What on earth do you have to put on your curriculum vitae to succeed at such an event? Presumably statements such as 'If I become your Member of Parliament I promise to dream up some really loony ideas that won't work'.

Public relations blunder of the year, with the teaching profession at any rate, was Tony Blair's assertion that thirty per cent of schools were failing. It meant that many people, both inside and outside the profession, did not pay proper attention to the detail of Labour's

119

proposals because of the headline treatment of what was an erroneous statement.

No government can run an education system without the support and respect of teachers, as the Conservatives have shown.

If we are to meet the many demands of the 21st century then of course standards and expectations must be raised considerably and incompetent teachers must go. But the Tarzan approach, especially if ill-founded, does not work, whereas partnership does.

I would give the 1995 teacher of the year award belatedly to Charles Warrell, who died in November at the age of 106. Better known as Big Chief I-Spy, Charles was a former teacher who had me and thousands of other parents chasing round the countryside trying to find a damned windmill so our kids could get their last ten points and finish their latest I-Spy book. He had the clever idea of turning his successful teaching methods, based on teasing children's curiosity and offering incentives, into newspaper columns and books.

I first met Charles when he was in his nineties. Later we went to his house for dinner. Dressed in an immaculate red smoking jacket, he told fascinating tales of teaching until the early hours.

He had wanted to call the successful I-Spy books the 'Learning about....' series, but his wife warned him that putting the word 'Learning' into the titles would produce zero sales. Since the series later sold 40 million books she was probably right.

When visiting a fellow village school head one day Charles heard a boy, asked by the head to perform some task, reply 'OK Big Chief', and that is how Big Chief I-Spy was born.

Charles was a triumph for the Third Age, the age of healthy retirement. He lived in Budleigh Salterton, or 'God's waiting room' as it is known locally. When he was 92 he bought an old oak chest, but no-one could tell him its age or its origins. He went to the library and sent away for books until he eventually tracked down its provenance. Ever the teacher he then wrote an article about it which was published in a national magazine.

When he was 102 Charles rang me up one day. 'What's all this about a new curriculum?', he began.

'Do you mean the national curriculum, Charles?', I asked, fascinated that a centenarian, retired from teaching for some forty years, should still want to know about his former profession.

'I don't know', he replied, 'I keep hearing about this new curriculum on the radio. What is it?'. I described it briefly and neutrally so as not to raise his blood pressure unduly.

'Is there anything about 'communication' in it?', he said, 'that's what's important for children, you know'.

I muttered about English and the 'Speaking and listening' attainment target. 'It doesn't sound like my kind of curriculum', he went on, 'but is it all written down in a little pamphlet somewhere?'

I hadn't the heart to tell him that it was indeed written down in a few dozen not so little pamphlets, whose sales to children and parents would be a tad less than his own 40 million.

For me Charles Warrell is the model of the future, an example of what today's children will do in the second half of the 21st century. It may be unusual now for someone to develop a fresh interest in his nineties, and still be curious about his former profession forty years after retiring from it, but for today's pupils it may be commonplace.

Hence the vital importance of giving children the best possible education for a very long future. With that cheering thought I wish you a happy and successful 1996.

Times Educational Supplement 5.1.96

Please write on one side of the planet

Did intelligent life come from Mars? Scientists have been looking at the microbes and bacteria buried in rocks that have landed on the surface of our planet from elsewhere. The evidence has been analysed, and the finest scientific minds have now confirmed that life on this planet is extraterrestrial and finely ordered.

There is conclusive proof that intelligent life did indeed come to earth from Mars. Those that passed to grammar schools came from Mars, those that failed the 11-plus and went to secondary moderns were from Jupiter. What is more, stupid life also originated extraterrestrially. Amazing but true. The microbes that got put on quangos, as political trusties and placemen, are actually from Neptune.

One day a sliver of protozoa, a blob of algae or whatever, swooshed down from space and landed somewhere in the Home Counties. Splat! Another day, a few aeons later, John Major was standing there eagerly inviting it to be head of some useless bureaucratic educational quango. Next time you walk on Bognor beach don't tread too heavily on any green squidgy bits. You might be squelching the prospects of a key political quisling in the year five billion AD.

From time to time journalists writing an in-depth piece (150 words) on the selection of Martians back in the old days, ring me up to ask me what the 11-plus was like in its heyday. Can I remember any of the questions? Indeed I can. I spent enough time practising them. At that time the identification of Martians was a simple business. There was 'mechanical' and 'mental' arithmetic, English, and 'aptitude'.

I always loved the 'mechanical' arithmetic part of the 11-plus. It was a surreal world of men digging holes and people filling up several baths, for no apparent reason. 'If it takes ten minutes to fill a bath with the plug in, and five minutes to empty it with the plug out, then how long would it take to fill five baths and empty them, one after another?' On Mars they were always doing this kind of thing. Indeed, since it had absolutely no point, it was regarded as the supreme existentialist act, so we Martians had a real advantage. Try it on Jupiter and all that water would probably have just turned to liquid hydrogen and oxygen, so the poor old Jupitans were clueless.

A few private schools that tried to get Jupitans through the 11-plus in return for large fees used to spend weeks with real baths, filling and emptying them, only to find that on the day the exam paper was all about men digging holes, so it didn't work.

Even today I am red hot at answering questions like 'If it takes seven education ministers seventeen years to cock up most of the education system, how long will it take one Prime Minister to screw up all of it?'

What in those days passed for 'English' was also very jolly. Candidates had to complete a series of well known phrases and sayings, like 'As old as the ....' We Martians would fill in the correct answer 'hills', while all the Jupitans would give away their origins by writing down 'rings round my planet'.

Once at our new school we tried to flash the credentials that had got us there. 'It's a long lane that has no turning, but then, the knowledge that every cloud has a silver lining is as old as the hills' we would opine in fluent Martian, only to get our essays back with the word 'cliché' scrawled ungratefully in the margin at regular intervals.

'What's a cliché?' a fellow bewildered Martian, guilty of the same crime, hissed quietly to me early in our secondary career. I had a quick under-the-desk look in my new dictionary. 'A trite phrase or saying', I whispered back, trying to sound as if I knew what I was talking about. 'What's 'trite' mean?', he asked. Another clandestine look at my little pocket dictionary. 'Hackneyed'. Pause as fellow Martian becomes more desperate. 'What's 'hackneyed' mean?' Another furtive rustling of pages. 'Something to do with taxis', I whispered. After that we Martians avoided the language of taxis.

I also loved the 'aptitude' tests. These were, in the main, verbal reasoning tests, with the odd figural item thrown in, just to confuse the Jupitans even further. "Apple' is to 'fruit' as 'carrot' is to ....?' It was a gift. 'Vegetables!' we Martians would scream, barely able to contain ourselves, only to get a thick ear from some hugely muscled early matured Jupitan who thought we were talking about him and his pals.

Every year, after the 11-plus results came out, there was what became known as the 'annual miracle'. In every secondary school in the country there were exactly enough places for the Martians and Jupitans in the area. This was amazing, because in some towns there were 15%

Martians and in others there were 30%. It made no difference. The number of places for Martians was always spot-on.

Parents of Jupitans and the young Jupitans themselves were often heartbroken and demoralised to find they were from Jupiter and not from Mars, especially when their elder sister or brother was discovered to be a Martian, but that's genetics for you. Still, it was a wonderfully successful system.

About 20% of the population was supposed to be Martian, including John Major. But back in the good old days only about half of them went to university. Now, we are often told, comprehensive schools, by putting Martians and Jupitans together, have ruined it all. Yet today nearly half the children in school get five high grade GCSEs and about a third of the population goes to university.

As a result of comprehensive education, a fair number of Martians and rather a lot of Jupitans are 'getting ideas beyond their station', as they say in taxis.

Times Educational Supplement 23.2.96

'If it takes four Jupitans to change a light bulb, how many Martians would fill a bath?'

Wherefore art thou a scholar, guv'nor?

As this year's testing season draws nearer, I wonder what lessons have been learned from last year's experience. A series of reports evaluating the 1995 testing programme has been published, so there is plenty of information about what went wrong.

For example, there have been claims that the number of children obtaining lower grades may have been exaggerated owing to a system of counting introduced by good old John Patten. Nuff said.

There were also a few problems with the Key Stage 3 English papers. The evaluation revealed that the best markers were teachers who were actually teaching English to 14 year olds at the time. Other markers without that recent direct experience were less accurate. Some of the 2,000 people who marked the scripts did not seem qualified to assess the performance of 14 year olds in English, and one person, apparently, ticked as correct a pupil's Shakespeare script that said Romeo used 'Simples and Metfords'.

On the other hand the marker may, of course, have been correct. It has been too readily assumed that the candidate should have written 'similes and metaphors' and that the marker did not spot the error, but this interpretation may be incorrect. Not many people realise that 'Simples and Metfords' really do exist, and are in fact less well known figures of speech.

A 'Simple', as its name suggests, is a facile self-evident remark, like John Major's vision of education for the 21st century presented to his party conference, when he said that children should learn to 'read, write and add up'.

This is a classic 'Simple', and someone who utters tons of them is known as a 'Simpleton'. The candidate obviously had John Major in mind and was thinking of the moment when Romeo says to his friend Benvolio, 'O, teach me how I should forget to think', a good example of what a simpleton like Major actually does.

A 'Metford' is a little more obscure. It is an expression of revulsion, the words of someone who is monumentally browned off. It originates from Maurice Metford, who lived in the 16th century and was the first English teacher to resign in a huff when he had too many test papers to mark. As he left his school, he uttered the words, 'Ye SATs are ye pits', which became the first recorded 'Metford'.

The candidate, therefore, was quite right in her answer. Romeo does use a 'Metford' when he says, 'Love goes toward love, as schoolboys from their books; But love from love, toward school with heavy looks'. Full marks to the candidate and examiner for knowing this unfamiliar term.

So perhaps we should not condemn too quickly the idea of having examiners who appear on the surface not to be qualified. One teacher has claimed that someone who marked the English scripts was a postman. He should have plenty of letters after his name then. I suspect he may be an English teacher who got fed up of being asked to 'deliver' the curriculum and decided to deliver letters instead.

He may, however, be just the right person to mark 'Romeo and Juliet' papers, especially at the end of the play, when Romeo, eager for news, asks his manservant Balthasar, 'News from Verona! – How now, Balthasar! Dost thou not bring me letters from the friar?' Who better than Postman Pat to understand why they didn't arrive till second post on Thursday, even though they had been posted at the main Verona post office with a first class stamp early on Monday morning.

There must be scope for people from many other jobs to mark national test papers. In fact, they could teach the plays as well, given the impending teacher shortage. How would the army tackle it? 'Right then, Year 9, attention! Standing up straight, facing me. You at the back, yes you Ramsbottom, you dozy little bleeder. Listen to me. Now tonight's homework is, write an essay entitled, 'Is Romeo a long haired Nancy who spent too much time poncing around under balconies, when he could have been killing people earlier in the play?'

Perhaps this year's Key Stage 3 English paper can even be conceived in such a way that having unqualified examiners would be a positive advantage. There could be separate questions for the members of different professions to mark.

Key Stage 3 Shakespeare Paper

Answer any three questions. The profession of the marker is in brackets.

1. Comment on what you found to be the most meaty bits of dialogue between Romeo and Juliet (butcher).
2. What are the advantages and disadvantages, in terms of resale value, of having a balcony put on your house? (estate agent).
3. Write a critical account of the way Romeo poisons himself (cocktail mixer).
4. When Romeo says, 'But, soft! What light through yonder window breaks?', does this indicate that Juliet's family should have had tinted glass? (double glazing salesman).
5. Does Juliet's speech beginning, 'O Romeo, Romeo! Wherefore art thou Romeo?' tell you anything about her eyesight? (optician).
6. Is the best way to get to Verona to go British Airways or Eurotunnel? (travel agent).
7. Discuss the scenes that take place in Juliet's chamber (plumber).
8. Find two 'Simples' and two 'Metfords' (politician).

Times Educational Supplement 8.3.96

Spigot-fanciers net trophies

'The Acme Spigot Company is proud to announce a new competition for schools. The competition is open to children in the 5 to 12 age range. Competitors should submit a sculpture made entirely out of spigots representing the concept 'Biodiversity in the 21st century'. The winning school will receive 100 free spigots a year until the year 2001, and the five finalists will each receive a voucher for 50 spigots'.

Some people are compulsive entrants to competitions and others cannot stand them. Yet there are more and more competitions for schools nowadays. Those who enter often feel: never mind what a spigot is (it's a bung actually), get the entry form and let us see if we can win resources, prestige or something for our hard-up school. If the spigots are of no use whatsoever, then perhaps we can sell them to raise cash.

Another bonus comes if the competition fits in neatly with the children's programme of work ('Spigots across the curriculum', 'The history of the spigot', 'The use of the spigot in modern technology'), because time spent on it will not then be wasted.

Having judged many of these school competitions, I have seen a wide variety of entries, ranging from the awesome to the awful. Submissions to the competition sponsored by the National Union of Teachers, based on the *Euro 96* football finals which take place in England through much of June, seemed uniformly high to me.

Here was a good idea, which capitalised on the considerable publicity there is for any major sporting event on British soil. Schools had to submit projects based on some of the sixteen countries with teams in the finals. This gave children the opportunity to find out more about well established countries like Germany or Italy, and 'new' countries, such as Croatia. There was an excellent set of imaginative responses, with posters, videos, displays. Children clearly enjoyed taking part, it fitted in well with their curriculum, and they will get more out of the football finals having learned about the countries.

Not all competitions work as well. Some attract very few entrants, even when valuable prizes are on offer. This is sometimes because the organisers have not taken advice about the subject matter, the timing, or the amount of time and effort required. On other occasions it is lack of publicity. I have seen competitions, especially at local or regional level, where the only decent entry won, much to their surprise, as they expected dozens of participants and found there were five.

It is worth giving careful thought to any competition you enter, as time can easily be wasted otherwise. For me the most important criterion for entering is that, if children have enjoyed what they do and found it worthwhile, then there are no losers. That said, how can schools get the best out of the experience? The first tip is to read the requirements carefully. If a fifteen minute video is required, then don't send in three hours of rambling, random-looking shots. The judges have to discount some entries simply because they did not send in what was asked for.

A second point is to present the submission as attractively as possible. This means that any artwork should be the best that children of that age can do, and any text the best they can compose. Drafting and redrafting a text, evaluating and presenting a finished product, are all part of the national curriculum in subjects like English, or design and technology, so getting children to aim high is time well spent. Even children's finest work may still look a bit rudimentary, but if it is the best they can do then that does not matter.

Another tip is to bear in mind that most winning entries have a touch of imagination about them. They stand out from the rest. Entries for some competitions can be pretty predictable, so any school that finds an interesting aspect, or an inventive solution, often has a head start.

In one competition, in which children had to predict the future, most entrants described some kind of ecological disaster. This was not surprising, as children care deeply about their environment and are very much afraid that it might be ruined by the time they grow up. What stood out, however, were the entries that portrayed this in some particularly graphic way, the ones that saw some positive possibilities, and those that used grim humour.

Most important of all is the enthusiasm that can be generated. When children and teachers are enthusiastic, this often translates into vivid and lively submissions. That is what makes most competitions worthwhile.

A small primary school in a rural area won a major prize in a national competition organised by a Japanese firm in which schools had to do something Japanese. The children and teachers got the whole village to join in their kite flying and other activities. Imagination and enthusiasm shone through and they won a crate of Japanese goodies, which led to even more celebrations. But it would not have mattered if they had not won, as they had had so much fun.

Times Educational Supplement 7.6.96.

My rabbit is ill and coughs just like this ...

There is something about doing research in primary schools that the textbooks never tell you about. Over the years I have watched hundreds of lessons in the pursuit of educational research. I have written books about research, including one on the very topic of classroom observation. Yet I have never properly addressed this vital topic. It is an omission I shall now repair.

The crucial subject about which every potential classroom researcher needs to be properly briefed is that primary classrooms contain children.

There, I knew you would be shocked. You see, if you are in the classroom to teach, then you are unambiguously in charge and your role is clear. But educational researchers are visitors, and the unwary can be completely thrown by the presence of children. The younger the class, the bigger the pitfalls, so I offer the following tips and hints to those embarking on such research.

The first tip is known as 'My rabbit's dead'. The earnest researcher, eagerly clutching notebook, pen, stop watch, checklists and any other trappings, has just got seated in a suitably discreet corner of the room, when the first of an army of five year olds, each keen to crawl a notch or two up the 'Speaking and Listening' Attainment Target, heads eagerly over to the innocent newcomer.

Forget your stopwatch and checklist, your objectives and schedules, your research council grant, or your higher degree thesis deadline. First you must hear the gory tale of the last death throes of Darren's pet rabbit, eventually consigned to the dustbin in a plastic bag, now at a thankfully unknown destination. By comparison with Darren, Roald Dahl is nowhere on the 'gruesome' scale. Just remember not to have eaten breakfast in future.

Tip number two is: 'Darren has a bad cough'. You know that familiar raking sound of a sack of coke being dragged over half a ton of ball bearings? Well get used to it, because it will be very close to your ear for the next couple of hours now that Darren has decided you are his lifelong sympathetic friend. Oh, and remember not to wear velvet or a thick ribbed sweater, as Darren never puts his hand over his mouth when he coughs, so as not to spoil the purity of its sound.

The third hint, for those still determined to carry out their research, if they have not by now forgotten both their topic and their proposed methodology, is: 'A scab'. The first time I ever went into a primary classroom to do research a fresh faced child came over to me and said, 'Shall I show you something?'.

Intrigued, I foolishly answered him in the affirmative, whereupon I was shown a livid scar of the kind that only six year olds knee-sliding on concrete tend to acquire. 'Miss has just told me off for picking it', he went on, pointing to the evidence, a hideously discoloured, half hanging sleeve of deceased skin. Will I be wanting a school lunch? I think not today, thank you.

Hint number four is: 'Locate the toilet'. Normally classroom researchers have no need of the little room, as the rigours of frantically noting down everything of significance leave little time for such luxuries as a widdle. Researcher Ronald King, who spent many an hour in infant classrooms doing the fieldwork for his book *All Things Bright and Beautiful?*, once wrote an account of how, desperate to write up his findings and avoid being quizzed yet again by the children, he would try to hide in the Wendy house. Even that was not a safe haven, however, so in the end he retired to the toilet, as it was the only available refuge. The staff were convinced the poor chap had a weak bladder.

The problems are usually worst during the first couple of visits. Children are very versatile, and they soon get used to someone who is happy to talk to them on some occasions, but is busy writing on others. In any case, if you are studying the behaviour of the class, then these little pieces of intimate sociology should have a legitimate place.

If familiarity does not do the trick, and you still need peace, then you can always try chewing garlic, or walking round the room carrying a large bag labelled 'extra work for children'. As a last resort you might even try wearing a badge marked 'OFSTED Inspector', but that desperate ruse will, I suspect, only work with teachers.

Times Educational Supplement 9.2.96

Cheesed off by the change industry?

A distinguished professor retired from a university a few years ago. On his last day in the university a keen journalist, notebook and pen quivering, came to interview the great man. 'After 25 years as head of this department, Professor Scroggins', he began, 'what would you say is your proudest achievement?'.

The professor mused for a moment. 'I think', he intoned, 'my proudest boast is that, on the day I leave, the course is exactly the same as it was on the day I arrived'. The bizarre belief that pride is to be associated with improving nothing at all during a career is, fortunately, unusual.

During the last six years I have directed three Leverhulme projects looking at classroom processes in the primary school.

The first studied class management, questioning, explaining and other important classroom skills, the second monitored teacher appraisal during the vital 1992 to 1994 period. My current project is looking at primary school improvement, especially in the field of literacy.

Trying to make primary schools better is a major industry nowadays, and there is no shortage of consultants eager to relieve them of half their budget to help them 'improve'. Yet much can be done 'in house', and within existing resources.

A great deal of time has been spent in recent years on structure rather than process, on how many boxes must be ticked, rather than how to explain concepts better. Instead of having time to improve what they do in their classroom, teachers have been buried under bureaucratic demands that sapped precious energy.

Professor John Gray, of Homerton College Cambridge, has analysed the first batch of school reports from the Office for Standards in Education. He reported that their recommendations were more to do with structures – improving the school development plan, changing the organisation – than classroom skill.

There are at least four important ingredients for improving primary education. The first is teachers' professional skills. A summary of research by American Herb Walberg and two colleagues found that what they called 'distal' factors, the American equivalent of national or local policies, were less influential on pupils' achievement than 'proximal' factors, those within each school. Of the school factors, the teaching skills of the staff came top. The most important of these was effective classroom management.

In theory, teacher appraisal was supposed to improve teachers' skills. In practice, as we found during the Leverhulme Appraisal Project at Exeter University, some 28% of teachers were only observed teaching one lesson, for as little as ten minutes, and slightly over half said they never changed what they did anyway.

The time and space to be able to help each other improve was what teachers most complained that they lacked. Teacher appraisal was required to be done in a hierarchical way, with the big cheeses appraising the little cheeses. Then along came a giant mouse, called 'Time Constraints', which gobbled lumps of both big and little cheeses, as heads and teachers were interrupted by numerous distractions. This is the Emmenthal cheese version of appraisal. Small wonder that many of the teachers we interviewed could not even remember their targets.

Time must be found to allow people to sit in on each other's classes or visit other schools, and there must be a focus. We found that very few appraisers knew much about classroom observation. Peer appraisal can only work if teachers know how to analyse teaching and learning. Improvement does not happen by accident. In our appraisal study, we found that if observers wanted teachers' respect, they had to have a proper professional's grasp of the age group and disposition of the children, the material being taught, and be able to offer fresh insights.

The second vital ingredient for improvement is the raising of aspirations and expectations. I often visit German schools, and do not share the uncritical adulation of German education, except in the fields of vocational education, which is superb, and the teaching of lower achieving pupils. One reason why German children outperform British children in number (though not in geometry, where we do better, so there), is the higher test scores from pupils of lower ability. German teachers' expectations of lower achievers are higher than I see in Britain, where it is almost as if we are resigned to being duffers at sums.

Third, teachers' morale and attitude to their craft is an important factor. It is hard to improve what you are doing through clenched teeth.

There are numerous examples of excellent leadership in primary education, but what is happening in Birmingham is of interest. Chief Education Officer Tim Brighouse has worked closely with primary and nursery heads to give primary schools more resources and to support teachers. Baseline testing of school beginners and trusting schools to set their own targets have replaced the whip and scourge approach of the Government.

The fourth feature of school improvement is the climate within the school. I have called schools with a positive attitude to improvement 'dynamic schools', on the grounds that there are positive forces at work.

After the mad whirligig of recent years, the operative word is 'judicious'. For Professor Scroggins, of course, 'judicious change' was the same as 'no change'. But as the 21st century dawns that cannot be the right recipe for the children who will spend most of their lives in its rapidly changing environment.

Times Educational Supplement 8.9.95

Childhood is catching

They say that after a while people start to look and behave like their pets. Cat owners curl up on the sofa and fall asleep. Those with pet Alsations look pointed and aggressive, while owners of bulldogs appear determined and jowly. People with dachshunds start waddling along and yapping.

Have you ever noticed how some primary teachers start to behave like the children they teach? Think of those reception class teachers who roll on the carpet and sing 'Incey wincey spider' just like five year olds, and then, once in the staffroom, spill coffee and biscuit crumbs down their front at break time, only to be told off by the deputy head for making a mess. It can happen to any of us.

I remember standing in a queue for a meal at a conference of primary teachers. One teacher at the back, feeling no doubt as peckish as year 6 at the end of a long morning, jokingly gave a bit of a push, rather like Darren Rowbottom would have done, and several teachers tumbled into each other. 'Now somebody's being silly', another teacher remarked disapprovingly. Two house points lost.

Perhaps it is the effect of spending hours having to deal with certain difficult pupils and then having a golden opportunity to misbehave yourself. Teachers driven to distraction by pupils refusing to do as they are told, must love getting stroppy with the head and seeing somebody else on the receiving end of perversity.

There is a psychiatric condition known as *folie à deux*. It occurs when someone who is sane lives with someone who is mad. The sane person starts to appear mad and imitates the behaviour of the person who is insane. One teacher had to cope with a wild seven year old, who was quite likely to run out of the school several times a day. The school was next to a busy bus route. The only way she got through assembly was if another teacher held him down while she bawled 'All things bright and beautiful' in his left ear, in the faint hope that he might join in. She confessed that, on her way home at the end of the day, she felt an almost irresistible urge to tip off policemen's helmets and run away.

I once taught a class of children that had quite a number of slower learning pupils. One of them, Wayne, always replied, 'I doant know' in his delightful regional accent every time he was asked a question. In desperation I asked him one day who Margaret Thatcher was, after she had been on television every second of the previous night. 'I doant know 'oo Margaret Thatcher is', was the endearing reply.

After a few weeks of this unfailing repetition, I found myself saying, in perfect mimicry of Wayne's plaintive voice, 'I doant know' to any question to which I did not have an answer.

One school in our locality found it had a problem with a term of abuse commonly used in the area. If any child appeared not to catch on immediately to a piece of classroom or playground conversation, other pupils would tap their forehead, put on a gormless expression and call out the word 'Digby', the name of the local mental hospital.

Patiently the head and staff explained, cajoled, coerced. It was unkind to mock anyone, they pointed out. Moreover, the people in Digby were not lunatics or retards, many were simply frail and nervous, needing shelter from the hurly burly of everyday life.

Gradually the pupils stopped calling out 'Digby' and the term faded out of use. Everywhere, that is, except in the staff room, where head and teachers alike cheerfully tapped their foreheads, put on a gormless expression and called out 'Digby' every time one of their colleagues failed in attention.

Times Educational Supplement 8.9.95

I'm glad you asked that ...

How do you investigate, disassemble and evaluate a product which has mechanical and electrical components? Search me guv. How do micro-organisms break down waste, or cause diseases? Er, let me think now... How do the valleys, rivers, multi-storey car parks, movement of goods and people in my town compare with a similar locality in Africa, Asia (excluding Japan), South or Central America? Just a second, it's on the tip of my tongue.

There is no need to worry about the answers to these searching questions. They all concern topics laid down by law for primary teachers to teach in just three of the national curriculum subjects they must cover at Key Stage 2, namely design and technology (knowledge and understanding – 'products and applications'), science (life processes and living things – 'living things in their environment') and geography ('places').

I know lots of primary teachers, so my problems are over. I can just ask any of them.

When the national curriculum was simplified, the assumption was that the ferocious demands on primary teachers' subject knowledge had been hugely reduced. The volume of words describing each subject had certainly been thinned out, and some of the content was slimmed, but much of it never went away.

Take as an example electricity and magnetism. Back in 1989 they had an Attainment Target all to themselves. These two dear friends were the whole of Attainment Target 11 in science, when Kenneth Baker wanted every child to be tested on every one of 60 or 70 different ATs.

In May 1991 it was proposed that there should only be five ATs and our twin chums electricity and magnetism were swallowed by number 5, 'forces'. That lasted until September 1991, when they officially became part of new number 4, 'physical processes'.

After Ron Dearing's slimdown 'magnetism' disappeared from Key Stage 1, though 'electricity' survived. Both are still alive and well at Key Stage 2, so demands on teachers' subject knowledge have not abated by much. Children still ask, as they did in 1989, 'Please Miss, what happens inside a magnet?', 'Please Miss, what is a battery made of?', 'Please Miss, if you stuck 500 batteries together and wired them up to someone's big toe, would he light up?'.

The vast stores of knowledge primary teachers are supposed to possess makes them fine candidates for Brain of Britain or Mastermind. In both programmes you can bone up on the knowledge, but it is the questions that are the killers. Even searching books and databases for answers is not easy if you do not know which sub-heading to look for.

The complicated topic 'floating and sinking' is a good example of this dilemma. Primary classrooms were once awash with children dropping pineapples, weights and oranges, with and without their skin, into bowls of water, while their teachers prowled round making notes on soaking wet clipboards. The topic may not now hold the position it used to occupy, but it is still there. Under the heading 'balanced and unbalanced forces', for example, children can still float objects in water to see what forces are acting on them.

It is not difficult to prepare activities, but when children's questions start to fly, then teachers' own subject knowledge can creak. Why do we float more easily in the sea than in fresh water? Simple. Salt water is 3% more dense than fresh water. How much lighter are we in water anyway? Easy peasy. As Archimedes discovered over 2,000 years ago, we become lighter by an amount equal to the weight of the water our body has displaced. All right then, clever dick, how do some insects manage to walk on water? What a facile question. It's all because of surface tension, silly. The inward attraction of molecules of liquid on the surface of the water to other liquid molecules, has the effect of forming a sort of skin over the water.

But suppose you don't know that 'density', 'Archimedes' Principle', and 'surface tension' are what you need to look up? And how can you best explain these ideas to curious primary pupils in terms they understand? It is not just a matter of subject knowledge, but of choosing suitable teaching strategies.

It is not surprising that most teachers have developed nifty footwork. One common ploy is Steinberg's Reflective Strategy, named after Sid Steinberg who turns every unanswerable question back on the class.

'That's a very interesting question, Damian, so for homework tonight, Year Five, I want to see if *you* can find out why wagtails wag their tails'. This tactic has the advantage of sounding pedagogically smart, as you can always, if asked, mumble something about 'ensuring that children learn to think for themselves in the challenging world of the 21st century'.

Another strategy is the Pickersgill Backhand Lob, perfected by Mavis Pickersgill, which dispatches thorny questions deep into the back of the court with, 'Thank you for that important question, Gemma. Now, whose turn is it to look up the answer in that shelf full of 1,000-page encyclopaedias at the back of the room?'.

Then there is the story of the Nobel Prize winner, who said to his regular chauffeur, 'You must have heard my standard lecture so many times, I bet you could deliver it and nobody would know you're not a Nobel Prize winner'. The chauffeur duly gave the lecture, word perfect, but to his horror someone stood up at the end and asked a mind-blowing question. He must have been an ex-primary teacher, as he answered, quick as a flash, 'That question is so simple even my chauffeur could answer it'. If all else fails, keep a Nobel Prize winner at the back of the room disguised as a chauffeur.

Times Educational Supplement 3.5.96